THE
STRATEGY
WORKOUT

SECOND EDITION

**Analyze and develop
the fitness of your
business strategy**

CYRIL LEVICKI

FINANCIAL TIMES
PRENTICE HALL

Pearson Education Limited

London Office:
Edinburgh Gate, Harlow
Essex CM20 2JE
Tel: +44 (0)1279 623623
Fax: +44 (0)1279 431059

London Office:
128 Long Acre, London WC2E 9AN
Tel: +44 (0)171 447 2000
Fax: +44 (0)171 240 5771
www.business-minds.com

First published in Great Britain 1996
Second edition published 1999

ISBN 0 273 64433 5

British Library Cataloguing in Publication Data
A CIP catalogue record for this book can be obtained from the British Library.

10 9 8 7 6 5 4 3 2 1

Typeset by Pantek Arts, Maidstone, Kent
Printed and bound in Great Britain by Redwood Books, Trowbridge, Wiltshire

The Publishers' policy is to use paper manufactured from sustainable forests.

About the Author

Dr Cyril Levicki started life in the tough streets of the East End of London. After leaving school he worked as a laborer to put together the money to start his own retail business. The businesses he has run range from a market stall in London's Brick Lane to manufacturing, wholesale, and retail companies.

After building a successful business career, he attended London University and studied economics and politics, as a mature student of 32. After graduating he was invited to teach managerial economics at the University. He was also awarded a scholarship to study for his Ph.D. at The London Business School. This he completed three years later and was invited to turn his research into an advanced strategy and policy elective for the MBA program, which he also taught.

Cyril was appointed a Visiting Professor at Queen Mary College soon after. He also served as Visiting Professor at Baruch College in New York.

Since 1983 he has acted as a consultant for many international organizations, usually helping chairpersons and chief executives to formulate or revise the long-term strategy of their businesses. He is usually retained for long periods thereafter to help these organizations change the behavior of their top teams to ensure successful implementation of the strategies they have devised.

For my son, Jeffrey,
and my wife, Phyllis.

Contents

Part Three: "Breaking Through The Pain Barrier"

Part Four: "Cooling Down Gently"

List of Case Studies

List of Figures

Foreword

Welcome to strategy and its supposed mysteries. There are fewer secrets to strategy than some would have you think – but enough to fill this book.

Why a strategy workout? Because learning to write a strategic plan is a basic skill required at every level of management. If you cannot do it you will not survive as a manager or a leader.

This book is designed to be user-friendly. There is a minimum of jargon and pseudo science. I try to specialize in common sense, aided by the good fortune of having spent the last 20 years formulating and implementing strategy with many leaders of mainly medium and large corporations and their teams. I do this through my consulting company, Omnia Consultants Limited which specializes in helping leaders formulate or change the mission and strategy of their business. The leader usually then retains Omnia to help him and his team understand and overcome the problems of implementation of the strategy. That ensures we design really practical strategies that work in the marketplace. We stay around long enough to be found out if they don't!

You can do the workout on your own or, even better, with your team. The book has a complete version of the workout in Part Four. You could try it out over a weekend to practice the skills. Then, complete the in-depth exercises in Part Two, together with your team, on an afternoon or a day away from the office. By the way, fill in the workout audits as you read them. It only works if you really complete the workout and discover what you do or do not know. If you do not fill it in you are more likely to miss an important subject you have not really understood properly.

All the workouts are also included on the CD accompanying this book, and can be completed, circulated and compared in electronic format.

Strategy can be fun, so, enjoy yourself. You cannot use your imagination too often at work. Creating strategy is one of the few times when you should be as imaginative as possible.

The objectives of the book

I have had to reduce the creation of new strategy to its barest essentials, to help leaders focus fast on the key factors they need to consider when deciding the strategic thrust of their organizations. The system has been tested in all sizes of organization and is intended to be learned and used in a minimum amount of time. Time, for senior managers, is always in short supply.

This book shows you how to achieve the same speedy strategy analysis used by successful executives. It also tells you how to develop leadership and managerial qualities to successfully implement your strategy.

A different way of analyzing strategy

Because my clients were always short of time, I had to devise shorthand methods to enable them to assemble the information they would need to take decisions about the strategy of their organizations. The "Strategy Workout" system evolved from that process. It has been continuously honed to be suitable for use in any industry and most circumstances. I noticed that my clients continued to use it long after they were taught the system. They usually took it with them when they changed employers or industries. I realized then that we had a general strategy analysis tool that would be useful to a wider public.

Implementation is much harder

As I became more proficient at helping clients devise new strategies, I also realized that the really difficult problems were not related to devising new strategies. That is relatively simple, once you get the knack. The killer problem is always strategy implementation. That takes a special chemistry of leadership, management, luck with the economy, skill and care in the development of your employees, and the controlled evolution of unique competencies in your organization. The only other key ingredient, in my experience, is **moral fiber**. Everybody in the business, at every level, has to believe that his company is providing great and valuable services or products, that it treats its people and its customers properly, and keeps to the rules of business and society in general. Organizations that do, succeed. Those which lack moral fiber eventually fail. That has become an essential part of my credo.

The final two chapters of the book are intended to help you to understand how implementation can go wrong, and how to get it right. Essentially it is people, working within the organizational culture of their business (the atmosphere in which people do their work), that are difficult to change. The very hardest people of all to change are leaders, usually because by the time they get to the top, their capacity to see the organization, its people or its strategic future with fresh eyes has diminished.

Leaders know that it takes many years of sensitive, insightful and inspired leadership to change the way people think, their values, and the way they behave. If they forget they might underestimate how hard it will be to change the strategic direction of the business. Leaders also need, alongside the strategy, a profound understanding of people. They have to judge, not only, what the underlying values of the behavior changes should be, but they must also understand how to communicate the different and changed behaviors and attitudes that will achieve the new strategy. They then have to decide which of their executives will help; who could help (once they are won over), and who will always be an impediment.

When I realized that I was seeing a constant pattern of similar difficulties with regard to implementation in fundamentally different organizations across a range of industries, I realized that it was time to tell that story too. That is Part Three of the book.

Acknowledgments

I should like to thank the following people for their help. My wife, Phyllis, who read and reread this work many times and told me when passages made no sense. My publisher, Richard Stagg, who is the only publisher who ever responded by fax within a week to say, "I'll publish your book." Also the many friends who have checked the book for content and common sense. Among those who read early versions and advised on improvements are Andrew Callaghan, (MD, ANC plc), Mr John Farrant (Chairman, William Sutton Trust), Mr Richard Gourlay (Journalist, *Financial Times*), Mr Ray Gudge (MD, Hays Distribution Group), Mr George Hazle (an MD of Exel Logistics), Professor Leonard Minkes (Emeritus Professor at Birmingham University), Mr Bert Morris (Ex-Deputy Chairman, National Westminster Bank plc), and Professor Derek Pugh (Emeritus Professor at the Open University). As always, all mistakes remain my fault alone. They have merely saved me from the worst.

To save endless repetition of "he or she" I have mainly used the male gender to denote both genders. I hope no female readers will be offended – I only wish there were more female managers and that it would be appropriate for reality's sake to use the female gender rather than the male.

Preface to the Second Edition

There is something gratifying when one gets to the second edition of a book, not least of which is that it proves that quite a few people bought the first edition. Furthermore, a considerable number of readers (from all over the world) have contacted me to tell me how to improve any further editions. I have taken all the sensible advice into account in this edition. Consequently, I have removed the first simplified version of the workout as many people felt it was superfluous. I have also tried to remove some of the sub-headings to make the book easier to read. An important change is the additional chapter (7) explaining how to analyze the value chain of the industry in which you are involved. I have also rewritten substantially the chapter on organizational structure (Chapter 9) to give easier guidelines on the key approaches to this most knotty of problems and have made many additions to Chapter 8 concerning the use of all your assembled data to actually create or devise the strategy from the preceding analysis.

I should like to thank Pradeep Jethi, my publisher at Financial Times Management, for his enthusiasm for this second edition. He took this project over from Richard Stagg, my first publisher, who has moved on to other responsibilities. It is not always the case that publishers embrace their predecessors' projects with relish. Many thanks are also due to Martin Drewe, my project editor. His responsiveness and kindness, allied with a continuous attention to detail, have often saved this edition from mistakes which would have had a detrimental effect on the quality we are aiming for. Thank you, Martin!

I hope readers and users of my workout methods find the second edition even more useful than the first. Thank you to all the readers who helped to improve it.

Dr Cyril J. Levicki, 1999

Part One

"THE WARM-UP"

Introduces you to the concepts of strategy

How to use Part One

The first part of the workout gives you the briefest possible
background information about the system and how to use it.

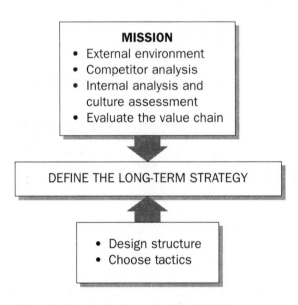

Figure 1 The strategic workout methodology

Introduction and Workout Test of Fitness

Strategy defined

Which organizations need strategy?

Who should analyze and who should implement strategy?

The process of strategic analysis looks at the external environment of the organization and the internal strengths, weaknesses, and culture to enable a strategic direction to be chosen. Once you know where you are going, you can "decide how to get there" (structure) and what choices of short-term tactics will make it happen.

"Lovers of wisdom must be enquirers into very many things indeed."

Heraclitus

How this book works

The book is intended to become a simple-to-use strategy handbook. It is based upon 20 years of practical strategic development work in organizations which needed to create and install new strategies. The workout system is currently being used by thousands of practicing managers.

The first ten chapters of the book set out a simple method for the analysis of strategy. This method has been refined by many years of practical work with managers and aims to ensure that one does not forget any important aspect of the analytical process as the strategy is prepared. Each chapter contains workout sheets on the subject of that chapter. These change from edition to edition because there can never be any "final" version. The subject of strategy formulation and implementation is evolving continually and requires constant updating.

The workout pages at the end of every chapter in Part Two of the book are simple, shorthand, forms which force you to think seriously and deeply about all the important questions you should consider before deciding what you wish your strategy to be. Do not be put off by the apparent simplicity or by the fact that they so often ask you to list just three or four of the most important aspects of the subject matter. Stating important data in a simple way is hard. For example, can you summarize the values of your business with just three or four words? Can you state, in two or three lines, the psychology of the leader of a competing firm? If you cannot, you must ask if this could be a problem. If you do not know your competitor's leader well enough, you will be unable to briefly summarize his or her strategic objectives. (Some senior managers cannot even name the leader of their competitors, never mind the strategy they might be using.) That is when you know you have more homework to do.

In order to give the reader an overall context of what the audits will cover, Part Four of the book contains a complete set of all the workout audits as they appear in the individual chapters of the first half of the book. You could try to complete them before you read the chapters in detail, to decide which areas you have more or less understanding of.

Most chapters contain short case studies and stories to illustrate the theory and how the practice can go wrong or right. Often the stories demonstrate what can go wrong, sometimes on apparently simple procedures. In other cases I give examples of unethical conduct or even moral turpitude and the reader will not be surprised that the perpetrator was unwilling to give permission for the story to be told. It is hoped that the stories will, nonetheless, give you insights and an understanding of how to implement the ideas contained within the book.

Occasionally you may feel a shiver down your spine as you read a story and wonder whether it is about you or somebody you know. The truth is these stories are about all of us because one cannot practice strategy and management without making mistakes. The qualities you need are those of continuous learning, relearning, and seeing the events which take place routinely every day – in a new light. At the very least, we should remind ourselves constantly of best practice. If you are not doing that minimum, then you have probably already begun to fail.

A definition of strategy

A strategy describes a set of objectives for any organization whether it is in the public or private sector and has commercial or nonprofit status. Strategy sets the objectives and the goals for the organization into a series of time frames to enable people to know what must be achieved, by whom, and when. The process of strategic analysis looks at the external environment of the organization and the internal strengths and weaknesses. The strategist then assembles the data to develop the objectives which will maximize opportunities for the organization.

Methodology and layout

The book is divided into four parts. This part (One) gives you an initial introduction to strategy. It should enable you judge how much you need to study particular chapters of the book to sharpen your understanding and capacity to analyze each specific area of strategy.

Part Two then describes the different stages of the strategic analysis process and indicates what data is needed and what thinking needs to go into the completion of each stage of the workout. The different stages of the process are:

- The mission, or why are we in business?
- Examining the external environment, or what's going on out there?
- Studying the competitors
- Analyzing inside the organization
- Organizational culture, or how do we really do things around here?
- Assembling an analysis of the value chain
- Defining the long-term strategy first
- Designing an organizational structure
- Choosing the short-term tactics.

Part Three explains the kind of problems which arise from the practicalities of strategy implementation from the angle of both organizational problems and leadership. It will show you how things go wrong (Chapter 11: Strategy is easy – implementation is hard) and how to put them right (Chapter 12: Getting implementation right).

Part Four is a final form of the workout system which will enable you to make your analysis of your organization with the benefit of the practice you have had in the previous sections of the book.

What type of organization needs a strategy?

An organization's strategy describes where it is going in the future. The diagnostic process of strategy analyzes the organization's total internal resources and external environment, and decides what and where will be its best opportunities to thrive. A strategy may have an overall objective of growth, staying stable or even diminishing the size of the organization.

> **An organization's strategy describes where it is going in the future.**

The strategy could move the organization totally or partially away from its current business interests. Whatever the direction of the strategy, the analysis must be carried out before taking important decisions. It is a fundamental tenet of this book that an organization must have a direction if it is not to wander aimlessly, buffeted and battered by any economic accident which may befall it.

The processes of strategic analysis set out here are user-friendly for any organization, whether it is in the commercial or the nonprofit sector; the same considerations apply and a similar level of knowledge of the external and internal environments is required. All organizations are chasing the limited resources of their sector of interests, be they charitable gifts of money or customers for products or services.

For a commercial enterprise, the components of competition are usually self-evident. The problem is the same for nonprofit organizations. A charitable foundation is competing for people's "gift capacity." If they don't appeal in a stronger and more timely way than other charities, they will lose – and so will the cause they exist to support. It is difficult to be objective about an organization's comparative situation in the marketplace. How does a successful organization decide that its current best-selling, market-leading ideas, products, or services are becoming redundant? What percentage of income should be reserved for research and development to seek replacement products? Possibly the hardest area to evaluate is what would be an appropriate level of investment in training and development of people in the organization.

The future is always uncertain but if the organization does not train people for that uncertain future then it can be sure that whatever future arrives, its people will not be ready for it.

Only high-quality strategic analysis can render these difficulties less difficult and the decisions more likely to be correct. The first step is knowing what the strategic analysis process entails.

Who should devise strategy?

Strategy should be devised by the leader of the organization. That may not be the titular head. Many organizations divide their leadership between the chairman and the chief executive. It will depend on circumstances who becomes the strategic business leader. That is the person who should devise the strategy.

Although Bill Gates, the founder and leader of Microsoft, the world's largest computer software business, is trying to become a more non-executive chairman, he still retains control of the strategic direction of the business, remaining in charge of decisions about which new products to develop and what new areas the business will invest in.

By comparison, at GEC, a multinational supplier to the engineering and defense industries, during the era of its former chairman, Lord Weinstock, the many large businesses it controls were run for individual business profit–ability. Their leaders were left to devise the strategy for their part of the business. The chairman was criticized for not leading GEC toward an integrated strategy which would enable it to be more than just the sum of its parts. Under its new chairman, Lord Simpson, attempts are being made to find an overarching strategy for the corporation which will ensure that the sum of the whole will be greater than the simple addition of the individual businesses.

The person developing the organization's strategy should not do it alone. Involving others is an essential part of the process of both strategic analysis and implementation, because getting others to participate also helps to encourage ownership and belief in the strategies that eventually emerge. Subordinates will believe more strongly in the strategy if they feel they have contributed to its formulation.

An additional reason for involving others is that one often finds that the most in-depth knowledge of the external world or the competitors is in the heads of people who are not necessarily high up in the organization's hierarchy. For example, salespeople who spend their time out in the field often know more about what competitors are doing than anybody else in the business.

> *The person developing the organization's strategy should not do it alone. Involving others is an essential part of the process of both strategic analysis and implementation.*

The best strategic leadership teams are those special relationships where the chairman and the CEO or managing director find a unique empathy which enables them to cover each others' weaknesses and accentuate each others' strengths.

A classic example of such a special relationship was Lord King at British Airways and his able managing director, Sir Colin Marshall. Lord King cared mainly about his vision of turning BA into the leading global airline. Marshall was content to be a loyal lieutenant and implement his leader's vision. Between them they built what became, in the early 1990s, the "best airline in the world."

Above all, the leader has to decide what his organization's good, indifferent, and poor skills and resources are. People who perform operational (rather than managerial) roles for the organization may have more objective views on these matters than the leaders might care to hear. If the leaders are capable of listening to the truth then they should listen to the workers on the shop floor in order to learn where the firm's real strengths and weaknesses lie.

Who should implement strategy?

The simple answer to the question of who should implement strategy is that *everybody should*. That is the only way the organization can move cohesively in one direction. It is a surprising and sad observation that many leaders are prepared to share their strategy with their shareholders (and even worse, their competitors) by publishing it in the annual report, but they would not dream of confiding it to their workers.

What to do now

Part Four contains a complete version of the Omnia Strategy Workout. That should be examined and completed first. If you are satisfied that it has enabled you to draw together most of the strands you need to develop your strategy you might decide you need to read only those parts of the text which your workout shows you want or need to understand better.

Where you feel you need more enlightenment on the meaning of any part of the workout, the text is designed to help you understand each separate subject area of strategy. Each chapter closes with the workout audit for the subject. I recommend that you complete these as you finish each chapter.

Readers should then reexamine the workout at the end of the book, in Part Four. If you have no further gaps in your ability to complete it, that will prove you are really strategically fit. Alternatively, you may decide you need to undertake further research and begin the whole process again. You are the customer and should use your purchase for maximum return.

I urge you to fill in your first strategy "workout" to test your organization's "strategic fitness." After that, please use this book according to the time you have available and the "fitness" or "lack of fitness" of your organization. A strategically "unfit" organization, like any sick, directionless human body, will struggle to survive and die young. I hope this book helps your organization to become or remain healthy.

Summary

The thesis of this book is that strategic analysis is simple. It is implementation of strategy that is difficult and, further, it is mainly the human element which complicates the process. Strategy is not value-free and must, therefore, take account of the beliefs and values of the people involved in the organization. This begins at the very start of the process of strategy analysis and is examined in Chapter 2: The mission statement; and again in Chapter 6: Organizational culture.

Strategic analysis is only the beginning of the important process of leadership of strategic change. Adapting the organization to fit new strategic needs defines the process of strategy implementation. That requires wise and sensitive insight into what motivates both large and small groups of people. Persuading them to adapt their behavior to achieve new and different objectives is the highest and most supreme aspect of the art of leadership. That is the subject matter of the final two chapters of this book.

Additional reading for this chapter

K. Blanchard and S. Johnson, *The One Minute Manager*, William Collins, Glasgow, 1990

R. M. Grant, *Contemporary Strategy Analysis*, Blackwell, Oxford, 1995

C. J. Levicki, *The Leadership Gene*, Financial Times Pitman Publishing, London, 1998

"THE MARATHON"

Understand the workout fitness test in depth

How to use Part Two

Part Two of the workout introduces you to each of the important processes of strategic analysis in detail. You will have discovered, if you completed the workout in Part Four at the end of the book, which aspects of strategy you need to improve your understanding of.

This part of the book will detail exactly what each section of the workout means and gives examples, where appropriate, to clarify exactly what is meant.

You may choose to select particular chapters from this section, depending on the workout test of the knowledge and understanding, which you have just completed. If in doubt, read the chapter. Complete the workout audits at the end of each chapter. Each iteration will improve your skill and understanding.

The Mission Statement
Or Why Are We in Business?

Setting the mission is the single most
important thing the leader does for the
organization. In so doing, he gives it a
purpose and direction.

"It is the first responsibility of top management to ask the question 'what is our business?'"

Peter F. Drucker

Definition of a mission statement

A mission statement is a general declaration of the purposes of the organization and the very long-term objectives that its leaders want to achieve. The best examples are written in an inspirational style to provide a focussed and motivating document for the organization's employees.

An organization's mission statement aims to be useful to the current employees, and all other interested people, such as applicants for work with the organization (for whom the mission statement may be the first introduction to the kind of operation they are applying to join), members of the financial community, current and potential investors, customers, and suppliers.

The leader may have to use different versions of the mission statement to communicate with non-employees, especially if it is written in an inspirational style. It might be preferable to communicate with the external stakeholders via a "mission statement to shareholders" or a "policy document for good supplier relations." These people are interested in entirely different aspects of the enterprise's existence. The kind of messages that should be contained in the mission statement may be contrary to the interests of the shareholders or suppliers. For example, shareholders may have shorter-term investment time horizons than the leader of the organization. They might want profit maximized in the short run and could be put off by a leader's mission statement relating to a ten-year plan, which involves short-term losses, or lower profit margins in order to reap eventual higher returns in the long run.

What is the organization leader's vision?

Setting the mission is the single most important thing the leader does for the organization. In so doing, he gives it a purpose and direction. Although leaders should consult with colleagues about the mission statement to gain acceptance and approval, they should be fairly sure where they really want to take the organization in the future.

A good mission should be sufficiently challenging to make people work more purposefully in a focussed direction, but not so daunting that it makes people feel helpless because the vision seems impossible to achieve.

President Kennedy's mission to get a man on the moon within ten years

One of the most quoted mission statements is that of President Kennedy when he set the mission for NASA, the American space agency. "We will get a man on the moon within ten years." This is often quoted as the ultimate mission statement because it was focussed, concise, had a clear goal, was made publicly and had commitment behind it. In those respects, it was an excellent example of the type. However, it also had weaknesses which ultimately led to catastrophic consequences. As a mission it made no commitment to quality, nor to the way employees should be treated. It also made no mention of any valid, long-term reasons for the mission. Ultimately, it was a "leap of faith" mission to keep the USA at the forefront of world leadership.

It could be argued that these shortfalls in the mission statement led to more people being killed in space before and after the moon landing. PR seemed to be considered a higher priority than looking after people.

The Kennedy mission statement was also too finite. It did not indicate any "next steps" after the moon landing. Certainly, the NASA organization seems to have gone nowhere since landing a man on the moon. Nor has it found another challenging mission to focus the organization's resources.

NASA has never taken advantage of its original lead in the industry which has now diversified into launching satellites into orbit for communication purposes. As a consequence of the Kennedy mission statement ignoring this potential future development, Chinese and French satellite-launching rocket manufacturers have beaten the Americans in that field for many years.

So, a mission statement which was too brief and failed to cover important issues such as care for employees and quality of product, lost the USA and NASA the opportunity to dominate a world industry of the late twentieth century, even though it achieved early total technological leadership.

What core competencies does the organization need to achieve the vision?

Core competencies are a group or set of skills that deliver the capacity to provide a service or product for the market. They will usually consist of technical and human skills. For example, Federal Express, which specializes in overnight delivery of small packages, has core competencies in: managing a centralized, physical hub system to maximize efficient package handling; motivating employees to deliver effectively whatever the barriers; and demonstrates pure logistics skills in the use of trucks and planes within a hub and spoke structure. Coca-Cola has a core human skill competence of managing a brand, dominating bottlers without ultimate share control, and maintaining the mythological power of its "unique flavour."

A mission which is intended to be particularly stretching usually requires the firm to learn new core competencies in order to achieve it. For example, Microsoft specializes in software to facilitate the use of computers. It wishes to increase its share of world markets in global communications highways. It will have to achieve mastery of some new core competencies in telemetry, networks, and communications applications before it convinces customers it is competitive in this field. But it will also have to take on new types of employees and find fresh ways of handling them. It will probably have to restructure its business to manage the different culture of its telecoms, consultancy, and Internet employees from its original software architecture specialists.

> *A mission which is intended to be particularly stretching usually requires the firm to learn new core competencies in order to achieve it.*

How does the organization treat its people?

A mission statement will often address how the organization treats its people. Some of this will be based upon the current style. However, it can also be aspirational in terms of how the organization wants to treat people in the future. This is not meant to be idealistic but realistic. For example, BT (British Telecom) created a new mission at the close of the 1980's, which made no mention of the staff. This could not have been an accident – its leaders are too sophisticated to have forgotten such an important con-stituency. The leaders knew they intended to reduce the size of the company from 250 000 to 140 000 people. It would have been seen as hypocritical and ill-conceived to make statements about how much the company cared about its people when it concurrently intended to lose (almost entirely through voluntary redundancy) about two in five of those employees.

How does the organization treat its customers?

It has become normal for most businesses to proclaim that they want to "delight" their customer; "the customer is supreme"; or "it is only because of the customer we are in business." However, very few actually organize their business around the possibility of enchanting their customer. Indeed so many businesses are mindlessly exploiting comput-erized, automated customer communications systems, that they are making it increasingly difficult for customers to talk to them at all.

The range of offers a business can make to customers can be more subtle than is often assumed. For example, some customers may require less service for lower prices in commodity industries. The mobile tele-phone industry woke up to this concept in 1998. It added 25 percent more customers in a few months by offering price controlled, prepaid pack-ages, in the UK. In other businesses, treatment of the customer may be the main differential between competitors. For example, Virgin Railways, in the UK, is trying to get premium prices for its First Class customers by offering "free breakfasts." Unfortunately, and simultaneously, they were failing, at the close of 1998, to achieve the prime requirement of all rail travellers, which is to have the trains run on time.

Many businesses base their research for new products and services upon customer focus groups. However, this can sometimes be mis-guided. For example, Akio Morita, the chairman of Sony, often claims that he would never ask the customer what they want because he con-siders it is his job to know what is possible and to then arouse the customer's interest in it. Customers can only tell manufacturers what they know – it is the supplier's job to create what is *not* known. In leading-edge industries or markets it becomes even more important that the mission statement should indicate to managers and staff which broad approaches it wishes them to adopt.

What will the organization look like in five to ten years' time?

The mission statement should paint a picture which enables employees to know in what direction the business is driving. They will draw sustenance from this picture of how their own conditions will improve as they provide better services from the business to deliver to their customers, to make the business thrive. It should show them the idealized future the leader wishes them and their customers to enjoy in the long term.

Philosophical paradox

Readers who are new to strategy creation should note that there is a philosophical paradox in drawing up a mission statement. In some ways it is strange to start the process of strategic analysis with a mission statement because it may not be too different from the long-term aim or strategy of the firm. If the mission statement contains the main objectives of the firm it should be anticipating what should evolve from the process of analysis itself. If you know where the firm should be going, as stated in the mission statement, why bother with the analysis at all?

It is because in all cases, other than brand new organizations, the organization starts the process of analysis with a history of what it has been doing up to this point. Leaders usually have some idea of what they want the organization to achieve and become. History itself will have created opportunities for the organization but will also have prevented it from attempting to enter other industries which might have proved more lucrative. National Cash Registers was small enough to become IBM, the world's largest computer concern, but IBM cannot become an oil company or a motor company, even if it wanted to do so.

It is a paradox that one must start with some conclusions. If subsequent analysis demonstrates that some of the long-term mission objectives are misconstrued or inappropriate, then this can and should be taken into account at a later stage of the analytical process.

When all the data has been collected and the organization is ready to decide what it wishes to achieve in its long-term strategy, one should reexamine the mission statement in order to judge whether any of the external or internal environment studies have produced important data that necessitates a change in the mission statement itself.

Mission versus vision statements

There are some esoteric books which define esoteric differences between mission and vision statements. This may be a useful distinction in academic terms. However, for the purposes of practitioners of strategy, the terms may be considered to be interchangeable. Both mission and vision statements refer to the very long term. They are statements of the longest-term set of goals of the organization.

The mission or vision statement represents the concept of what the organization's leaders would like the organization to become. It is usually produced by the organization's leaders – who ought to have the best judgment skills, since it is their prime responsibility. If it is delegated to others, there is the danger that the organization will not achieve unanimity on its mission.

An organization's long-term goals should be consistent, should not contain contradictions, nor target too many directions at a time. It cannot follow a thousand dreams, just a few. Setting the long-term objectives is the most important task and duty of the leader of an organization. These objectives may be couched in terms of "market share," "highest quality," "lowest costs," "ubiquity," or "dominance" of particular markets. They may be written in terms of the markets the organization wishes to dominate or the types of products it will specialize in. Whatever the method chosen to encapsulate the message, the mission or vision statement should indicate where the business is heading in the long run.

> An organization's long-term goals should be consistent, should not contain contradictions, nor target too many directions at a time.

The mission statement is a *dream* only in the sense that it requires imagination, ambition, and sensitivity from the leader about what is achievable. It should *not* be *dreamlike* in terms of achievability. If it does not look feasible, it will not be credible and, eventually, it will just be ignored.

Below are two mission statements. The first is that of BT in the early 1990s as it prepared to become one of the leading telecommunications enterprises in the world. The other is that of Trust House Forte (THF), an international hotel and leisure group, which was taken over in 1997 by Granada plc, a larger entertainment, leisure, and hotel company in the UK, after having unsuccessfully tried to defend its performance.

The British Telecommunications (BT) Mission

- To provide world class telecommunications and information products and services.
- To develop and exploit our networks at home and overseas so that we can:
  - meet the requirements of our customers;
  - sustain the earnings growth of the group on behalf of the shareholders; and
  - make a fitting contribution to the community.

The Trust House Forte (THF) Mission

- To increase profitability and earnings per share each year in order to encourage investment and to improve and expand the business.
- To give complete customer satisfaction by efficient and courteous service, with value for money.
- To support managers and their staff in using personal initiative to improve the profit and quality of their operations while observing the company's policies.
- To provide good working conditions and to maintain effective communications at all levels to develop better understanding and assist decision making.
- To ensure no discrimination against sex, race, color, or creed and to train, develop, and encourage promotion within the company based upon merit and ability.
- To act with integrity at all times and to maintain a proper sense of responsibility towards the public.
- To recognize the importance of each and every employee who contributes towards these aims.

Two questions arise from these two mission statements. Do you think the THF mission statement failed to give its leaders and employees a sense of urgency and focus about its strategic position (which, in turn, made it vulnerable to a takeover bid)? The other mission, that of BT (which is a much larger business than THF) is highly focussed. Does that mean that all the key people in the business know exactly what they are at work to do?

Additional reading for this chapter

R. Adams, J. Carruthers, and S. Hamil, *Changing Corporate Values*, Kogan Page, London, 1991

A. Campbell, M. Devine, and D. Young, *A Sense of Mission*, Hutchinson, London, 1990

G. Hamel and C. K. Pralahad, *Competing for the Future*, Harvard Business School Press, Boston, 1994

E. Jacques, *Time Span Handbook*, Heinemann, London, 1964

T. J. Peters and R. H. Waterman, *In Search of Excellence*, Harper & Row, New York, 1982

THE MISSION WORKOUT

Complete the following mission audit questions.

What is the vision of the leader of the organization?
(Where is he taking the organization in the long run?)

_____

_____

_____

What core competencies need to be obtained?

_____

_____

_____

What will the organization look like in five years' time?

_____

_____

_____

Examining the External Environment
Or What's Going on Out There?

What is meant by "outside the organization?"

Analysis at the international, national, and subnational levels

Advice on which areas to focus upon

Ways of controlling the external environment

Factors which must always be looked at in the world outside the organization

The scan of the external environment should include anything that is happening outside the organization within its industry, and in other relevant industries. It should also include all the other factors anywhere in the external environment that might affect the organization's interests.

"Learn to see things backwards, inside out, and upside down."

From the Tao Te Ching of Lao Tzu, fifth century BC

Start the strategic analysis outside the organization

Chapter 2 described how the first job in a strategy workout is to decide what the long-term mission of the organization is. Having done that, the next step is to move mentally outside the organization and look at the external world. The scan of the external environment should include anything that is happening outside the organization within its industry, and in other relevant industries. It should also include all the other factors anywhere in the external environment which might affect the organization's interests. These might range from politics (and relevant politicians), the law (particularly in regard to taxation and legislation controlling industry standards), and (where relevant) the dangers of political turbulence in countries which might affect the organization.

It is advisable to start the analysis outside the organization because at this stage of the process you might still be capable of objectivity in the strategy workout. Once you get involved in analyzing the nitty gritty of your own business, your objectivity is more likely to be eroded and you may begin to *search* for "data" which fulfils your preformed views rather than objective, sometimes unwelcome, information arguing against your preferred mission. Thus, when you scan the external horizons outside the organization, you are likely to look at them with a subjective eye which will seek corroboration of what you want to believe, rather than objectively examining interesting external facts and events that might really affect your business.

Start the workout on the exterior of the organization. This offers some small chance of avoiding the natural human tendency to look only at those things that corroborate our own prejudices. The best strategists avoid this problem with cold, calculated self-control and ruthless questioning of every key assumption. Few leaders are capable of such rigorous resolution. This is an entirely separate phenomenom from that when a leader, after the analysis, has to demonstrate strong beliefs about the chosen destination for the organization. They have to "sell" that solution to their people, to ensure the organization's success. Even so, when leading well by clearly delineating the strategic direction, a good leader will never be prevented from knowing, objectively, where the greatest weaknesses and biggest vulnerabilities of the strategy lie.

A slight case of AIDS

A large and eminent design company wanted to become international because it saw its clients becoming global. It wanted to follow suit, believing that there was strategic logic in a "design firm" going global to mirror the global enterprises it was working for in the oil and food industries. My client wanted to buy a concern in the USA for about $20 million. During the process of due diligence (the period when a bidder for a business examines the books in detail, to check that there are no hidden business risks before closing the deal with cash or shares), the auditors discovered that one of the two founding partners, and a key player in the business, had AIDS. Upon discovering this they asked for a medical report. The selling partners managed to find a doctor who was prepared to say "It is only a slight case of AIDS." So determined was my client, against advice from many of his executives, to buy the company and become international, that he went ahead and bought the company, in spite of the medical fact that people with AIDS usually die. Sadly, although unsurprisingly, the sick partner died a few months after his company was acquired. The company went to pieces, became bankrupt, and eventually bankrupted the parent company too.

The moral of the story is twofold. Firstly, a correct analysis of the external environment would have informed the strategist that large firms which were going global, were usually happy for their small firm suppliers to continue to supply them from their home bases – so he did not really need to develop an international presence. Secondly, the power of self-delusion is great, even to the extent of persuading oneself that a "slight case of fullblown AIDS" is even a remote possibility. It explains why I recommend that the strategist start the analysis *outside* the organization.

What external environment do we mean?

The external environment is infinite. You are only interested in the relevant data, predictable events, and states of the environment which appertain to your business. But, in looking at them objectively, you need to see what is interesting and important rather than only those phenomena which might be advantageous to your organization. One way of avoiding too easy an interpretation of how these events will affect your business, is to analyze the environment from the point of view of your closest or most feared competitor. If it can affect the business there is no reason to assume that you can avoid danger – unless you have specifically constructed a policy to neutralize the exposure. Whatever method you use, try not to interpret or devise strategies and tactics until you get to that stage of the strategic design process. Defining the long-term strategy or short-term tactics is still quite a long way off.

The environment can be classified under the following headings:

- International, national, and regional markets
- Economic trends
- Political events
- Legal, social, and demographic factors
- Particular expectations and tendencies of the industry in which you are involved.

Let's examine the key criteria within these classifications in turn.

International markets

A key strategic aspect of managing international markets is the problem of communication. Once an organization becomes international it has to develop special methods of communicating and skills to overcome the potential hazards. The first hazard may be language. That is immediately followed by problems of differences in culture, law, and national attitudes. The capacity to communicate is no longer a constraint given modern telecommunications; however, excessive telecommunication may increase the possibility of bad quality management through attempts to overcontrol.

A further complexity of international strategic growth is the management of physical distribution. Frequently, domestic businesses dominate their home markets through control of the physical distribution system. This might be well disguised. An intruding business from abroad might sink millions of dollars of capital investment before realizing that it cannot penetrate the market. Furthermore, the industry may be at a different stage in its development and have different patterns of competition and distribution. This makes it particularly hard to form valid opinions about the power of domestic competitors, which often have unpublicized connections with government officials and influencers who can distort the rules and regulations in favor of the home competitor. Japan and France are just two outstanding examples of this phenomenon. Just being on home territory is a powerful aid to the incumbent firm.

> *Frequently, domestic businesses dominate their home markets through control of the physical distribution system.*

When examining international or global markets one needs knowledge and understanding of different national characteristics. These will differentiate the form of demand for products in each country. They will indicate the basis upon which it may be necessary to differentiate and "localize" products and services when trying to penetrate markets.

Differences between the cultures of countries are sometimes startling and surprising. It is far too convenient in international organizations to take real cultural differences for granted and fail to remember in how many subtle ways one has to manage each country differently. Fons Trompenaars, in his book, *Riding the Waves of Culture* (Economist Books, 1993) points out the variety between different nationalities. For example, he found that 91 percent of Swiss respondents to his questionnaire would *not* write a false personal review, even to help a friend, whereas only 17 percent of Yugoslavs would have a similar inhibition; 97 percent of Australians prefer to be left alone to get on with the job; in Egypt only 32 percent like to work alone. Most Italians (71 percent) would openly express feeling upset at work; only 17 percent of Japanese respondents would share their feelings of being upset.

One should also be asking other important questions about the external environment. Has any particular country where your organization is involved become less stable politically? Is it part of a strategic alliance? Should you continue trying to penetrate a particular country or cut your losses? Are there new growth opportunities which did not exist before? In the 1980s I did some work with a senior officer (sadly, now dead) of Ultramar Petroleum. The business had substantial contracts to mine LNG (liquified natural gas) in Indonesia. He always enjoyed reminding me that Indonesia seemed far more stable than normal democratic states, which had elections every few years causing strategic upheaval every time the government changed. When I continued my objections to working with a corrupt dictator, he repeated that President Suharto had ruled Indonesia for many years and looked likely to do so for many to come. As far as he was concerned that constituted much greater political stability than existed in the UK or the USA. Unfortunately, his strategic analysis failed to take into consideration that the only way to remove a corrupt, totalitarian dictator, in the absence of a democratic system, is by means of a revolution. It duly came, in 1998. The disruption and devaluation of accumulated assets was much larger than any normal democratic election result could ever bring about.

National markets

The difference between analyzing the strategic environment when a business is national, rather than international, is massive. National markets need to take into account the variations in local customs and geographical distances in terms of the costs of distribution. Strategically, the difficulty with being a national specialist is that you are vulnerable to international competitors of whom you may be unaware when dealing with just your local environments. Although the scale of national business is intrinsically different from that of larger, international businesses, it is no less important to understand when national or international legislation, politics, and trends (both social and economic) may actually affect your local business. This problem is accentuated with the increase of large political agglomerations, such as ASEA (Association of South East Asia), the EU (European Union), or the American Continental political alliances.

For example, although you may be running a small country hotel, national and international standards of hygiene and food preferences will still affect your business. Similarly, you may have a thriving small and locally famous business, but that will be entirely irrelevant for a major international hotelier who will see the local and the national market in a different context. The small operation's fate may be rendered meaningless in a national or international context and scale. A business will need to take the potential large competitor into account. This is not reciprocal for a large international business. The large operator will not usually need to reciprocate by taking the small operator into account in its calculations.

Putting the organization into an international context

The leadership of a large national cable concern was having great difficulty in getting its managing directors to understand why they had to become more customer focussed; the organization was losing over 40 percent of its customers each year – and it was much harder to win customers a second time than it was to retain them with good service the first time around

They called a conference of the top 30 directors. The organization's original objective had been to dominate the German market for cable services by the year 2001. For this reason, the managers felt there was plenty of time to worry about "being nice to customers," eventually.

The organization's leader decided to put the matter into context. Instead of dominating Germany he had decided that, with the oncoming deregulation of the whole European market, he wanted the organization to dominate Europe instead. Thus, rather than aim to have a 50 percent share of the 80 million person German market, he wanted to dominate the European market with a 350 million population. This completely changed the attitude of his team. They suddenly realized that there was no time to "play" at learning to get customer service right . They had to get it perfect now, as well as lock up the whole German market, to be ready to take advantage of the much greater opportunity in Europe!

Regional markets

Many of the key warnings about nationally oriented organizations' vulnerability to much larger international rivals apply to regional businesses. The key advantage for the regional business is to thoroughly understand local conditions, as well as market differentiators and distribution channels. There will also be idiosyncrasies of local politics and planning regulations. There may be special rules about property. There often exist opportunities to close off access to vital resources or rights. The local business must use such knowledge to exploit the few advantages which its smaller size confers.

A German food discount corporation became aware of the high profit levels enjoyed in the UK food retailing industry. These margins are high because the market was dominated by two large retail suppliers, Tesco and Sainsbury's. The German corporation tried to set up retail discount stores in the UK, but every time it applied for planning permission, Tesco and Sainsbury's combined to raise objections on planning law grounds with every local authority, where permission was requested. Because the domestic lawyers had superior knowledge of all the possible reasons for refusing or granting permission, they managed to frustrate the newcomer enough to dishearten it. The German corporation gave up after several frustrating years of legal red tape. Eventually, the UK government changed its policy of granting planning permission for all new out-of-town supermarkets – thus ensuring the continued domination of Sainsbury's and Tesco's duopoly. That will leave the two businesses to slog it out between themselves. By the end of 1998, Tesco had won most of the first few rounds.

Economic trends

Ultimately an organization cannot buck the economic trends of its industry. Bryant and May was originally a Swedish company which set out to try and achieve a monopoly in matches which were used mainly for lighting fires, gas stoves, and cigarettes. Unfortunately, by the time it had almost achieved its objectives, cheap disposable lighters were so ubiquitous that the monopoly was worth almost nothing in extra profits, because a viable substitute product was available.

The concept of the product life cycle is often relevant here. The theory is that all products and services go through a life cycle of four stages:

- *Stage one* is the introduction of the new product to the market. It is likely to be bought only by a few innovative, and probably wealthy, people who like to be "avant-garde" in trying new products. The first stage is rarely profitable for the supplier(s) because the costs of development are high.
- The *second stage* is of rapid growth when many more suppliers emerge to make the product. These manufacturers have been able to overcome the barrier of the original inventing organization often having patented the manufacturing process. This stage is often unprofitable at the beginning (because there are too many suppliers) but becomes profitable toward the end as some suppliers exit the market.
- The *third stage* is known as maturity. It is usually profitable as the market matures and continues to grow but with far less competition as the less efficient suppliers drop out of the industry.
- Finally, there is the *fourth stage*, a period of decline as the market becomes saturated with the product and the main sources of customers are people needing replacements or new entrants into the overall market. Figure 2 illustrates these concepts.

Examine the trends for your business sectors. Which section of the product or service life cycle do your products fit? If you wish to grow your business you need the largest possible range of products and services in the second stage for growth and the third stage for maximum profitability.

It is possible to migrate from old, mature, or low-profit-margin industries into high-growth, high-value-added and high-profit industries. This takes a great deal of strategic planning and decisive, intelligent strategy

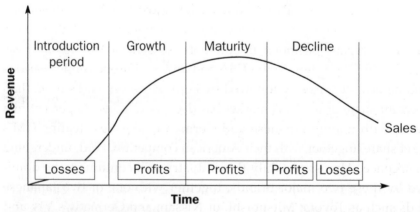

Figure 2 The product life cycle

implementation. There is never any shortage, under modern banking conditions, of capital available for investment, as long as intelligent strategic analysis has taken place and the organization's leaders demonstrate a strong probability of successful implementation of change, growth or migration to the new industry. A classic example of a successful migration is that of Reed International which moved from a low-profit, mature industry of paper and packaging into the high-profit, growth industry of international publishing and data processing.

> *It is possible to migrate from old, mature, or low-profit-margin industries into high-growth, high-value-added and high-profit industries.*

Businesses which lead their industry

Every industry, whether local, national, or international, tends to have one or two outstanding leading organizations which are seen as the vanguard in that industry or field. In information technology, for many years, IBM dominated and was synonymous with the computer industry. Now, everybody in the computing industry has to take account of Microsoft. In hotels, Hilton, Marriott and Holiday Inn dominated in the USA whereas Forte and Meridian were dominant in Europe. In international telecommunications, ATT was a dominant global player with a particularly strong brand in the USA, whereas Europe has been dominated by domestic telecommunications groups such as Deutsche Telecom, France Télécom, and BT. However, in international telecoms, WorldCom has become a player in just a few years. In Europe, the scene is still dominated by the domestic PTTs (State-owned post office and telephone systems). However, the mobile operators are beginning to challenge the fixed line company positions. In automobiles, General Motors (GM) has had a dominant position in the USA and around Europe (under various brand names). It is closely followed by Ford. However, GM's more than 50 percent share of the USA market has decreased to just 33 percent in a decade, with mainly Japanese and German businesses stealing GM's market share, together with their American competitor, Ford, undergoing a resurgence. Almost certainly this industry will continue to be dominated by these two major brands, together with one or two Japanese brands such as Toyota, Mitsubishi, or Nissan, and Germany's VW and BMW probably also surviving as global players.

Availability of capital

Between 1950 and 2000, the world will be seen to have become increasingly dominated by large global and national brands. As we move into the twenty-first century with lower barriers to entry in many industries, increasing availability of capital, and increasing dispersion of technological know-how, we will see more industries fragmented. This will create greater opportunities for entrepreneurs to develop niche markets in regional, national, and global industrial sectors.

However, there will be a contrast between very large corporations using economies of scale to maintain their size-related advantages compared to small enterprises using nimbleness and energy to compensate for their lack of scale. The large organizations will have the disadvantage of the costs and difficulties of administering a large operation; the small will have the disadvantage of seeming to have to fight for scraps off the giant's table. Occasionally, the small operator will win in the marketplace and begin to develop the disadvantages of size. For example, consider what happened to Apple Computers as it became a large corporation in the 1990s. It failed to adopt the policies and norms of management of a large corporation. Because it persisted in trying to run itself inappropriately with the management tools of small business, it lost most of its market share and its lead as an innovator in computer architecture to its competitor and, eventual, master, Microsoft.

Every industry has leading exponents of the skills of that industry. Somehow, these businesses are able to make more money out of the same turnover or have lower costs than most others of the same size. It is vital to study those competitors and understand the source of their competitive edge. The words I hear most frequently from losers in any industrial battle are "those fools must be losing money if they are selling at those prices." I have found from my experience as a consultant to "the fools" who were losing money, that they were making even more profit at the same price than the competitors who thought they were fools. Few people or organizations are prepared to lose money when doing business. Some, with extremely long-term strategic vision, are prepared to lose money for a short while, but only in order to gain strategic market share.

For example, the cable industry in the UK has been losing money for over a decade. It is prepared to make these losses because it foresees a bonanza, once the enormous investment costs of installation have been recouped. People in the industry have to hope that the external circumstances do not change too much and that they will be able to make their profits eventually. However, if satellite technology develops interactivity capacity and can squeeze more lines on its bandwidths, the cable industry may be denied the profits it currently sees coming its way.

Where is the profit in your industry?

The first question any good strategic analyst must ask when the "workout" first begins is, "how does one make profit in this industry or business?" You should compile a list of the different branches of the business. Some of these will be profit makers while others just cover their costs; frequently, there will be others which lose money. When doing your preparation for the workout, be sure to have a clear list, in order of profit merit, from best to worst. For example, a typical list for a business in the transport industry would be that set out in Figure 3 below.

Obviously, from the details of Figure 3, any business in the transport industry would want to move its main source of revenue into the

Business type	Profit margin %	ROCE† %
Logistics management	7	30
Warehouse management	6	25
Vehicle management	5	20
Management of drivers	4	24
Contract hire (vehicles)	4	14
Contract hire (people)	3	18
Warehouse space	3	10
Truck rental	3	8
Engineering service	2	14

•These figures are illustrative and are not intended to reflect reality in this particular
   market
†Return on capital employed

Figure 3 Example of profitability in the transport industry*

"Logistics management" sector. Many firms in the industry concluded that if they added the word "logistics" on the side of their trucks it would enable them to make increased profits. Naturally, as most of them did nothing to increase their skills or competencies in IT or learn more about how to provide "logistics management services" to their customers, the main effect of their changes was to increase profitability in the *truck painting* industry.

The prime question should always be "is the business capable of moving to new, more profitable sectors of the industry. Does it have the know-how, will, and cash to develop or buy what's missing?" It will depend on the condition of the business whether the organization chooses or is forced to stay in the poorer profit sectors. Furthermore, the difficulties of exit will be key. That is described next.

The height of entry and exit barriers

A key factor in industry profitability is whether it is easy to get into the business or difficult to exit. To concentrate on entry first, businesses or industries which are easy to enter are normally less profitable and offer low returns on capital. Ease of entry implies that it does not take much capital to start up in that industry; or the technological barriers are low; or the human skills required are not complex; or, finally, that there are no legal barriers to entry.

For many years the easiest form of business to enter in the UK was retail confectionery, tobacco, and newsagency. Consequently, these small businesses had low margins and (frequently) unskilled entrepreneurs running them. Gradually, throughout the last half of the twentieth century, corporate multiples bought up the prime sites in that industry which has matured into an oligopoly, led by companies such as W. H. Smith. Unfortunately, W. H. Smith forgot it was a conglomeration of small businesses. It tried to turn its small stores into large, High Street retail outlets. This turned it into a business which had lost its mission in corporate life. It had, by the end of 1998, spent several years attempting to find a new strategy.

A key factor in industry profitability is whether it is easy to get into the business or difficult to exit.

Another cause of low profitability in industries is the difficulty of exit. This often refers to heavily capitalized industries, where firms have very large amounts of capital tied up in single process machinery that cannot be used for other purposes. The cost of scrapping such large amounts of capital is so high that it is easier and more economic to continue to run at a loss than take an expensive write-off and exit from the industry. The effect applies, however, to almost any long established business with any property assets held on long-term leases. The premises tend to be, more or less, customized to the specific business's needs. The greater the cost of conversion of the premises to suitability for other industrial uses, the higher the exit barrier.

Is the industry different in each national market?

Some industries are differentiated between countries. For example, distribution systems are rarely the same from country to country. It is vital to understand how your industry differs in other countries if you are intending to undertake international expansion. Often a skill that you value the least in your home market is exactly what is prized abroad. For example, Unilever sells soap in India off the back of trucks as a cash business. This is not much different to methods it dropped in Europe 50 to 70 years ago.

Similarly, there will be areas where a firm has a leading edge in its domestic market which it believes will simply transfer abroad. But the leading edge may turn out to be commonplace in the targeted country, at least in an oversupplied sector. Alternately, the organization's skills may be seen as too innovative in the foreign market and it would probably cost too much to persuade the new market to accept a different approach.

One of the great fallacies in the strategic analysis made by American business concerns wishing to enter the European market is that they believe that Europe is a unified, integrated market of 350 million people. Federal Express and several American banks have come to Europe with that belief. Their argument is that if they can run an integrated operation for a 250 million population in the USA, then an integrated firm looking after the 350 million population of Europe can achieve even better economies of scale and returns on

> *One of the great fallacies in the strategic analysis made by American business concerns wishing to enter the European market is that they believe that Europe is a unified, integrated market of 350 million people.*

investment. In fact, Europe is not an integrated market but highly differentiated from country to country. The differences are caused by language, legal systems, and cultural inheritance. Consequently, operators like Federal Express found it very difficult trying to come to terms with the economies of scale which the European market *apparently* offers, but which are just not there.

Federal Express

In the USA, Federal Express has built a USA-wide business with a hub and spoke system, providing an express small parcel service overnight from any part of the States to any other part. They fly all their traffic on their own planes into their hub in Memphis, Tennessee (chosen for its excellent flying weather). They fly everything out the same night to every city and town in the States and finish the delivery by truck. Federal Express came to Europe thinking that a similar hub and spoke system, which had worked in the USA, would work for Europe. It even hoped for greater efficiency as it calculated that the European market was larger than that in the USA. Unfortunately, for Federal Express, Europe is not one large nation like the USA but a collection of highly individual nation states which have many means of not cooperating, no matter what European Community law dictates. After a few years trying to make the UK the center of a European hub, Federal Express had to exit from the UK with an exit loss of over $80 million, as well as accumulated losses of many millions more. It continues to trade country to country in Europe but has, for now, been forced to forego the dream of a European replica of the American system.

Many European enterprises have made a similar mistake in the opposite direction, believing that America is one integrated market with a common English language. In fact, every North American state has its own traditions and distribution systems, as well as idiosyncrasies of language and law. A car can be sold in New York or the mid-west, which will be illegal in California because of California's tight emission control laws. Food additives which are permissible under European legislation may be inadmissible in the USA. Above all, employment conditions in both Europe and the USA differ from country to country and state to state. Dixon's, a leading retail supplier of electrical and photographic products in the UK and France, took over an American chain of electrical goods shops, brand-named "Silo," which its leaders thought was involved in a similar industry. Dixon's skills in the UK are discount retailing, branding, and controlling distribution chains. It found that few of its UK skills were transferable and it began to lose money to an extent that was becoming a hemorrhage. It had to take a large loss on its investment and exit with its tail between its legs from the USA, retaining a minority share in Silo Holdings.

The politics affecting your industry

Politics in any country normally reflect the social trends being adopted by the population in general. After all, politicians are only selling people's hopes back to them, in return for the right to exercise political power over the voting population. It is, therefore, vital to be thoroughly aware of the social and political trends which could affect your industry. Social trends, such as the aging of the population, an increase in demand for a pollution-free environment, or a social ethos demanding more ethical behavior toward employees and customers, are merely the more obvious manifestations of political legislation reflecting social demand and fashion.

Furthermore, social trends and political legislation can become tools available to the organization as a means of achieving strategic intent. Persuading politicians to pass legislation to set standards and rules in an industry is one of the tried and tested methods of eliminating weaker competitors from the marketplace. It is a practice often engaged in when an industry enters the high growth phase of the battle for market share (see section on product life cycles on p.53). Most fast-growing, emerging industries indulge in such behavior.

Once an industry becomes mature, one often finds that the survivors are particularly adept at influencing public and political opinion.

Once an industry becomes mature, one often finds that the survivors are particularly adept at influencing public and political opinion. In Europe, the pharmaceutical industry has traditionally been adept at lobbying. In the USA, lobbyists for the car industry are renowned for their capacity to achieve legislation which raises barriers to competition.

Similarly, and increasingly, retailers are affected by legislation on how they must treat their employees, the permitted hours of work, the minimum levels of pay and the standards of care that must be given to employees. All legislation increases the cost of being a member of an industry. Once the major slices of the market are carved up among a few leading organizations in an industry, then it is standard practice to raise prices to create the high levels of profit which attracted them to the industry in the first place.

Legal factors affecting your interests

It is useful to periodically examine the particular legislation which affects your industry or interests. Is it fair? Has it become outmoded and in need of amendment? Are there organizations competing with you which are not playing by the same rules? In which case, does that give them an unfair advantage? BT has complained that it is not allowed to compete with AT&T in the USA markets for telecommunications as freely as AT&T can compete in the UK. This situation places a strategic disadvantage upon BT which it must overcome by persuading its official regulator to even out the odds, or persuading Parliament to change the rules or by influencing US officials to redress the perceived, unfair legal obstacles. Transco, the international, UK based gas distributor, competes with many other utilities which are also using its facilities to enter Transco's own market. Unsurprisingly, it may be tempted to pursue policies which disadvantage its competitors. Unfortunately, for Transco, the industry regulator, Ofgas, is used by its rivals to force Transco to play fair with them at a cost to its own competitive interests.

Influencing legislators and legislation

The means of creating legislation which is favorable to your business is to be an influencer at local or national government level. That means developing and maintaining relationships with local and national politicians. One also needs to develop relationships with civil servants as well as be invited to participate in the inquiries and advisory groups that normally create new, or change existing, legislation. There are very few organizations in leading positions in industry which do not try to achieve representation on such committees.

In the USA this requires even more persistent and comprehensive lobbying because the different constituents of national power are separated. There one has to run lobbying campaigns with both the legislature for new laws, and the Executive, for the application of any particular legislation. Finally, a business must "use" the legal system to attempt to get a favorable interpretation of any laws which have been legislated.

Demographics in the external environment

With increasing globalization, wages and conditions of employment also become more international. There will always be a tradeoff in certain industries on the costs of transport and the distribution of product, with regard to weight and size. However, as services, low-material element goods (such as entertainment, information, and education), and other high value goods become major constituents of the economy, suppliers will seek the lowest cost supplies, wherever they are in the world. Thus, national wage and income levels become controlled by international prices and cost standards. Software can be written in India, China, Ohio, or Oxford. The only factor affecting the purchase of such services is the absolute cost to the commercial operator, as well as the quality of the service supplied. If service and quality are equal, then the only remaining factor is price.

Increasingly, the world is dominated by absolute price competition. People are just another resource needed to create the mix to produce a service or product. This has led to a diminution of the power of trade unions in countries where, previously, they were able to dominate particular industries. One thinks of the Teamsters in the USA, or the National Union of Miners (NUM) in the UK. In earlier days such unions dominated politicians and the managers in their industries. In the UK they have even been known to bring down a government (the strike by the miners in 1973–74 certainly made a major contribution to Prime Minister Edward Heath's loss of power). Such unions nowadays have less power to affect their industries. It is only too easy for General Motors, Ford, or Toyota to turn to a country where dissent is minimal, or with the lowest trade union power, or the lowest cost per unit of labor supplied.

Expectations, trends, and tendencies in an industry

This refers to the concept of whether the organization is in a growth or mature phase of its key products' life cycles. Some industries increase or decrease in fashionability, depending on the environment. For example, during the 1980s, conspicuous consumption was a key feature of a perceived successful economic era. Demand for conspicuous consumption products such as champagne, restaurant eating, brand name clothing, and prestigious sports cars was fashionable and profitable.

As the recession of the early 1990s tore into previously prosperous segments of the population, businesses that had enjoyed fashionability were overtaken by events and saw the demand for their products fall drastically. This had severe effects on their profitability and capacity to survive, as they had geared up with economies of scale for the earlier, successful era. Thus BMW and Porsche ran into severe problems because they expanded and invested in manufacturing plant to take advantage of the fashionable 1980s, an era which was followed by a severe decrease in demand for their type of luxury products. The French wine industry has been suffering throughout the early 1990s. Many suppliers of leisure services and holidays have become unprofitable.

On the other hand, industries which have been unfashionable, such as public transportation, environmental pollution control, and the supply of vegetarian products are becoming more fashionable, profitable, and desirable.

From a strategic point of view, one needs to be sure that apparent increases in demand for an industry's products are really sustainable in the long term and not merely fashionable. If you are only following a relatively brief trend, fashion should ensure that you are gearing up for short-term demand in a way that does not involve you in long-term capital costs or economies of scale. Of course, a business may choose to migrate from industries which have cycles of fashionability and into a more stable environment. This will become increasingly difficult in the new millennium as we see even more rapid changes in the rate of economic growth, while simultaneously witnessing a decrease in the total length of product life cycles themselves.

Additional reading for this chapter

R. M. Grant, *Contemporary Strategy Analysis*, Blackwell, Oxford, 1995

G. Hamel and C. K. Pralahad, *Competing for the Future*, Harvard Business School Press, Boston, 1994

P. Q. Quinn, *Intelligent Enterprise*, Free Press, New York, 1992

THE EXTERNAL ENVIRONMENT WORKOUT

What are the most important economic factors in the organization's domestic market?

1 _____ 2 _____

3 _____ 4 _____

What are the most important economic factors in markets abroad?

1 _____ 2 _____

3 _____ 4 _____

What are the most important political factors likely to affect the organization?

1 _____ 2 _____

3 _____ 4 _____

Which legal factors affect or could affect the organization?

1 _____ 2 _____

3 _____ 4 _____

Which current demographic trends may affect the organization's workforce?

1 _____ 2 _____

3 _____ 4 _____

What are the trends in demand for the organization's main services or products?

1 _____ 2 _____

3 _____ 4 _____

Is there any key political legislation which could affect your industry(ies)?

1 _____ 2 _____

3 _____ 4 _____

How to Study the Competitors

Where are the dangerous competing organizations?

Where are the dangerous competing people?

Where will competitive attacks come from?

International, national, and regional competitors

Analyzing individual competitors

The analysis of who you consider your competitors to be also defines the industry and business you think you are in.

"The saying, 'There are many enemies' applies when you are fighting one against many ... . The spirit is to chase the enemies around from side to side, even though they come from all four directions. Observe their attacking order, and go to meet first those who attack first ... . Always quickly reassume your attitude to both sides, cut the enemies down as they advance, crushing them in the direction from which they attack."

From *A Book of Five Rings*, by Miyamoto Musashi, 1645

Introduction

Competitor analysis became almost a generic term during the 1970s and 1980s to replace the more complete strategic analysis which the rest of this book outlines. Other writers on strategy include competitor analysis under the "general external environment" analysis. It is really too important not to merit a separate chapter on its own.

The analysis of who you consider your competitors to be also defines the industry and business you think you are in. Thus, if you are in the insurance business, but only look at broking companies, then you are really defining yourself as a broker, not an insurer. Similarly, if you are in the business of air travel in and around Europe, you may consider your competitors to be only other airlines. However, if you define your business as "transporting people around Europe," you will define yourself as belonging to the transport industry with specific interests in European transport. You will also look at competitors in the ferry, train, and road transport industries.

It also follows that if you are considering a strategic transformation into a new industry, then you should be able to name the organizations with which you will compete in that new sector. The competitor workout at the end of the chapter will show you whether you really understand that industry and its key players, both at the company, business, and industry level. Do you know them as deeply and profoundly as you should if you are about to enter the industry?

One of the sillier mistakes that many organizations make about their competitors is to underestimate their ability. In addition, most organizations have areas which they consider to be sacrosanct, where they are not prepared to give ground or allow competitor intrusion under any circumstances. If you wish to attack a competitor, then it is wise not to arouse that competitor's most aggressive competitive spirits by invading its particular, sacrosanct territory. If you do decide it is appropriate, then it should not be an accident. When attacking especially sensitive strategic territory, it should be a deliberately aggressive act. You do it when you consider your organization to be so strong that you choose to deal your competitors a psychologically mortal blow – and you should be utterly sure it will be a knockout!

Top industry performers

As one of the first steps in your competitor workout you should be able to name the top few performers in the industry in which you are competing or wish to compete. By and large, the top one or two will be very well known, but it is vital not to miss numbers three and four, especially if you are not among them. For example, in the grocery industry in the UK most people would name Sainsbury's and Tesco but what would be your guess for numbers three and four? In the USA most people would say IBM is still the leader in the delivery of computer hardware and among the leading players in the delivery of computer software. But, who ranks next? Is it Microsoft, Apple, Compaq, AT&T, or a host of others who are large players in both the computer hardware and software industries?

The global entertainment industry is particularly fascinating as we enter the new millennium, because it is promising to be one of the world's largest industries. Businesses within it are merging, devolving segments, forming new alliances, and searching for opportunities as each business decides on its specific range of interests in the creation of entertainment materials, the ownership of the means of distribution (cable, television, cinema, satellite) and the need to achieve geographical coverage of some or all of each of these aspects of the industry. For example, Rupert Murdoch, a global mogul and owner of News International, a media company, has decided to specialize in one form of distribution (satellite) but is trying to do it in every geographical segment of the world, namely, Europe, Australasia, and the Americas. He is also specializing in two segments of infotainment (information and entertainment), production with newspapers (everywhere) and film (Fox studios in the USA). This makes his businesses difficult to compete with because he is strong in every aspect of the media industries. Furthermore, he has established a reputation for strong and aggressive tactics, with high levels of skills in lobbying and relationship management with political leaders all over the world. Anybody in any part of the media industries must take account of News International, wherever they are established.

Other important national competitors

An organization does not necessarily have to be a leader in its industry for it to be important at national level. Thus, although the organizations cited above, by dint of their global size and reach, were leaders in the computer industry in the UK and abroad, Amstrad Computers was for some time an important UK national player in the provision of personal computers to the British retail market. Similarly, British Airways (BA) is a large player in the international air travel market. It has several national level competitors, each of which may be important only on a few international routes. For example, British Midland is a national player, with just a few international routes. However, BA has to decide whether British Midland expanding into destinations around Europe is a specific threat which needs dedicated competitive action. Defining who the important national players are and profoundly understanding their competitive profile is important. ValuJet is a UK-based air journey business based on low costs for low prices. It started life as a national carrier but has rapidly moved into the European market, gaining market acceptability. This has forced BA, the UK-based global airline, to respond with its own "no frills" economy line. BA now has the problem of running a service-laiden, high price/high service airline in one part of its

> **Defining who the important national players are and profoundly understanding their competitive profile is important.**

business together with a contradictory, low price/low service airline in another. Which culture will prove to be the stronger? One possible outcome could be BA's reversion to the high price/low service air carrier it was in the 1970s.

The most dangerous people in competing organizations

In all circumstances organizations are much more important than any individual within them. This is more true the larger the organization grows. Nevertheless, one should also recognize the importance of specific individuals in some organizations or industries. In some industries particular individuals are gifted, dominant, and dangerous. Recognition that they dominate their industry is probably a sensible approach to analysis.

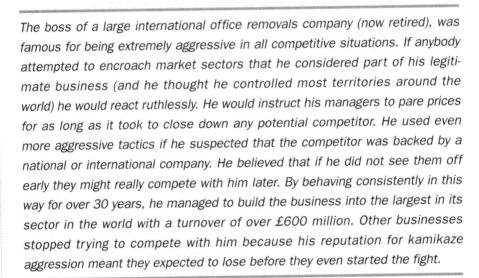

The boss of a large international office removals company (now retired), was famous for being extremely aggressive in all competitive situations. If anybody attempted to encroach market sectors that he considered part of his legitimate business (and he thought he controlled most territories around the world) he would react ruthlessly. He would instruct his managers to pare prices for as long as it took to close down any potential competitor. He used even more aggressive tactics if he suspected that the competitor was backed by a national or international company. He believed that if he did not see them off early they might really compete with him later. By behaving consistently in this way for over 30 years, he managed to build the business into the largest in its sector in the world with a turnover of over £600 million. Other businesses stopped trying to compete with him because his reputation for kamikaze aggression meant they expected to lose before they even started the fight.

It is important to know these dangerous people, both for their aggressiveness and their intelligence. You may decide to work in ways that do not draw their attention toward your organization. That is usually the wisest course of action. You might attempt to buy them onto your side in the industry. Whatever strategic approach you choose, it is always dangerous not to recognize them or take their predictable attitude into account.

Important regional or local competitors

Most national and international organizations take their strategic decisions on the basis of objectives such as market share domination or lowest price operator. They sometimes forget that local markets can be dominated by small regional enterprises with important local skills. They may be better connected to local infrastructures, have better access to more resources, know the local politicians and/or journalists better, or merely have a local reputation which is more important in the region than the national or international brand which the larger company may use to dominate most of its markets. It is important, at the very least, that the local managers of the larger companies be aware of the local enterprises which are firmly established in their own regional territory.

The many sources of competition

The first and keenest competition comes from other organizations within the industry. There are four further sources of potential new competition.

The first source could come from those businesses which are currently customers of organizations in the industry and who might be tempted to try to buy their suppliers or create their own supply service (usually because they believe their supplier is making too much profit). This is known as *integrating backward*. A typical example of this would be Sainsbury's or Tesco in the UK integrating backward and managing their own goods deliveries, rather than having them supplied by a third party logistics firm. Tesco actually bought a transport supplier to the company, to obtain greater control over its own physical distribution.

A second source of new competition could come from current suppliers to the industry. To continue the analogy above, a haulage or logistics company could find itself competing against truck manufacturers. This, in fact, happened during the recession in the early 1990s. Truck manufacturers, who had the manufacturing capacity to produce a high number of trucks (no matter what the demand curve), entered the haulage industry to develop a commercial outlet for the trucks which they were unable to sell directly to their customers in the logistics industry. This type of strategic behavior is known as *forward integration*.

Thirdly, one has to look across the entire commercial horizon for competitive danger and scan the entire business environment for any operator which might want to enter the industry. At present, there is a vast amount of *spare capital* slushing around the world. Any good business idea will find capital funding. There are also many mature, high-profit companies which are accumulating cash faster than they can invest it in their own industries. Such companies, with large cash balances, are loose cannons and could enter any growth-oriented industry they choose.

For example, Microsoft, now a global computer software business, has accumulated so much wealth (in 1999 it was holding around $20 billion in cash), that it has bought stakes in businesses in cable hardware, property, Internet, and film industries. Even if it doesn't stay in them all, it can use its capital and its shares (which have a higher value than most competitors) differently to most other businesses. It could also create havoc before it exits from any position it decides not to persist with. Similarly, in the United States, AT&T and the baby Bells, spun off after the breakup of the monopoly in the 1980s, have positive cash flows of several billion dollars per annum. Many of such organizations are using this cash to enter the "megamedia" industries of the twenty-first century.

Most organizations with spare funds are likely to:

- purchase businesses which they perceive to be making excess profits;
- move into industrial sectors where their core competencies can be exploited to take advantage of growth opportunities;
- buy businesses which add synergy to their strategy.

The last source of competition comes from the *threat of substitute products*. In a new age of technological innovation, no product or service is immune from the threat of substitution, even when a business thinks that it has a patent to protect its unique features. Pharmaceutical companies are notoriously litigious in their attempts to protect their patents. However, their competitors frequently find some substitute to compete with the best selling products of their rivals.

In the USA, WalMart appears to have merged the skills and techniques of the best retailers and physical distribution businesses. Others will find ways to replicate what it does and offer a substitute. Microsoft appears to have created a virtual monopoly with its "Windows" architecture for personal computers, but its monopoly will be broken one day, by a substitute product. It is inevitable when a business is evidently making high, virtual monopoly profits, that it will attract rivals who wish to share or grab its excess profits. Microsoft is currently fighting a battle in the US courts to protect itself from those competitors.

In a new age of technological innovation, no product or service is immune from the threat of substitution.

Figure 4 The many sources of competition

Adapted from Michael Porter, *Competitive Strategy*, Free Press, 1980

They assert that Microsoft is using its wealth to create rival products to theirs – even giving them away to prevent its rivals from getting a grip on Microsoft's marketplace.

Individual competitor profiles

You will see at the end of this chapter that the competitor audit sheet has two pages. The first covers the previous headings in this chapter under "General Competitor Analysis." The second is headed "Individual Competitor Profile" and will enable you to test your understanding of particularly important competitors by completing a workout audit of a few simple details about them. You should complete a separate "Individual Competitor Profile" sheet for at least the top four performers in your industry, whether you are international, national, regional, or local.

The questions in the competitor workout are simple. However, you might be shocked when you discover how many of these simple questions you may not be able to answer accurately. In that case, you should take the trouble to research the details, either from the competitor's annual general report, in-house knowledge within your organization (particularly from your representatives and salespeople), or from other sources in the industry, within local or national government records, the academic world, the news media, or professional data providers.

It is advisable to keep those records fully and continuously updated. A key feature of this part of the workout is knowing the competitor's leader. This does not automatically mean the chairman or the chief executive. There may be other influential people in that organization who are affecting its strategic direction. This is why you should know their psychology, vulnerabilities, and whether they are satisfied with their current position in the industry. If they are going to take new strategic initiatives, you need to have considered what they are likely to be. Even more importantly, you ought to know what that most influential person cares about most deeply. Armed with that knowledge, if you are going to make any strategic moves, you will be able to predict whether your competitor is likely to retaliate or not, and how.

Finally, you should make a judgment about your competitor's most important strength in its business. You also need to know what your competitor's most important weaknesses are. If you are going to mount a strategic attack, it should be aimed at exploiting those weaknesses rather than combating the strengths. The general rule is that an organization should only show strategic aggression when it is sure to win – and preferably against the weaknesses, not the strengths, of their competitors.

> **The general rule is that an organization should only show strategic aggression when it is sure to win.**

A successful example of this behavior was the attack by BIC, a French firm which specializes in "throw-away" everyday goods, such as pens, lighters, and safety razors. It attacked the American market for cheap razors, much to the annoyance of the mighty Gillette, which dominated the American razor market. Gillette threatened to start making cheap pens to flood the French market. It was an idle threat. The real retaliation came when Gillette launched its own version of a cheap throw-away razor, which it then introduced to the European market. However, BIC has remained the dominant supplier, based on its special competence in making relatively low quality but fair value-for-money products.

A less successful example of such an attack was that of Amstrad Computers on the market for personal computers in Europe. Amstrad never understood the need for quality and professional back-up in the PC market. Consequently, it was unable to sustain its attack and after a short-lived success was beaten back from the market by much more customer-oriented manufacturers, wholesalers, and retailers such as Compaq, Apple, IBM and other low price but adequate, Far East "own label" suppliers.

When you have completed the competitor analysis for your organization, think about what your competitors would write about your company if they were doing a similar analysis on you.

Additional reading for this chapter

M. E. Porter, *Competitive Advantage*, Free Press, New York, 1985
M. E. Porter, *Competitive Strategy*, Free Press, New York, 1980
P. Q. Quinn, *Intelligent Enterprise*, Free Press, New York, 1992

THE COMPETITOR ANALYSIS WORKOUT

Current Industry Competitors

Under each category below, put in the names of companies or people where appropriate. Regard this as a simple measure of your knowledge of the industry.

Which are the top performers in your industry?

1 _____   2 _____

3 _____   4 _____

Are there any other important national competitors?

1 _____   2 _____

3 _____   4 _____

Who are the strategically most dangerous people in competing organizations?

1 _____   2 _____

3 _____   4 _____

Which are the important regional or local competitors?

1 _____   2 _____

3 _____   4 _____

Which are the current customers most likely to integrate backward?

1 _____   2 _____

3 _____   4 _____

Which are the current suppliers most likely to integrate forward?

1 _____   2 _____

3 _____   4 _____

Any organizations which might enter the industry?

1 _____   2 _____

3 _____   4 _____

THE INDIVIDUAL COMPETITOR PROFILE WORKOUT

Complete one of these for each important competitor mentioned on the previous page.

What is the competitor's company name? _____

What is their annual revenue? _____ **and their annual profit?** _____

What is the name of the competitor's leader? _____

What is their psychology? _____

Is the competitor satisfied with their current position in the industry?

Yes/No

If not, what strategic moves do you think they will make?

_____

_____

_____

What action from your organization will provoke the fiercest retaliation?

_____

_____

_____

What are the competitor's most important strengths?

_____

_____

_____

What are the competitor's most important weaknesses?

_____

_____

_____

Organizational Self-Analysis

From SWOT to SNOT

How to turn weaknesses into strengths

Concentration on strategically important strengths

The importance of remaining objective when examining your organization

A slightly more complex way of conducting the internal audit of the business can be achieved by adding a simple extra line of analysis called "neutrals." This is an entirely novel way of analyzing the SW part of the classic SWOT analysis.

"It is a humiliating consideration for human reason, that it is incompetent to discover truth by means of pure speculation, but, on the contrary, stands in need of discipline to check its deviations from the straight path, and to expose the illusions which it originates."

From *Critique of Pure Reason*, by Immanuel Kant

Strengths, neutrals, and weaknesses (SNW) analysis

SWOT analysis is one of the best known tools in the strategic or marketing toolbag. Almost everybody seems to know the phrase and many use it. It stands for:

Strengths
Weaknesses
Opportunities
Threats.

There is one problem with this analysis. In spite of its beguiling usefulness, it is just a bit too simplistic to be of profound value. This method is usually used by strategists by applying the opportunities and threats analysis to the external circumstances of the business and the strengths and weaknesses headings to examine the internal skills of the organization. The method can give a fast but superficial view of what the external and internal environments appear to offer the organization in terms of strategic opportunities.

A slightly more complex way of conducting the internal audit of the business can be achieved by adding a simple extra line of analysis called "Neutrals." This is an entirely novel way of analyzing the SW part of a classic SWOT analysis. It is, therefore, a small claim of originality by the author that his key contribution to strategic theory has been to change the concept of SWOT to SNOT! (or, to be technically correct, SNWOT).

ABZ Truck Rental: turning a weakness into a defeat

How can the addition of one extra line add so much to a comparatively simple analytical tool? Because it removes the possibility of a classic mistake that many executives make when devising the strategy for their business. It may be clear to them that the organization is weak in a particular skill which is vital to the successful achievement of the strategy. They, therefore, "wish" the weakness into a strength. Thus executives often find themselves including a weakness as a key part of the strategic plan, even though this may cause the whole strategy to fail.

For example, ABZ was a market leader in the truck rental business in the UK. However, it had poor information technology systems and mainly used a manual system. Its managers knew that a simple business such as truck rentals should be able to take advantage of computerized booking and administration systems which were commonplace in slightly more complex businesses such as airline ticketing. Unfortunately, the leaders decided to develop their own "in-house" software rather than buy it as a ready-made package. Seven years and £20 million later, ABZ had failed to install a single information technology (IT) system; its competitors, such as Ryder and Transfleet, had caught up and were overtaking it, and its market dominance was gone.

Seven years earlier the strategy had included IT excellence as part of the assumptions for the strategic plan to remain market leader. The false premise (that with good IT they could dominate the market and grow) led, *inter alia*, to the corrosion of the whole strategy. Firstly, they threw money at the problem, which was wasted; secondly, they could have chosen a different, more apt, set of criteria upon which to base their growth; and, thirdly, they lost seven years during which their competitors lapped up all the growth which ABZ could have had.

Information technology is a common weakness

Of course, those ABZ managers were not fools. Nor are the many hundreds of leaders and managers who have tried to build strategic intent upon their organization's IT weaknesses during the 1970s, 1980s, and 1990s. They realized that they had made assumptions which were not based on fact. To compensate, they would throw large amounts of corporate resources at the IT weakness, in terms of both personnel and capital, to try to remedy what they knew was a fundamental flaw in the strategic analysis and their ambitions for the company.

Unfortunately, business weaknesses do not change that easily. If turning weaknesses around were just a matter of throwing money at the problem, no profitable businesses would ever go wrong. What tends to happen is that weaknesses develop over time and go on being just that – a fundamental weakness in that business's skill range. Thus, when businesses make the key mistake of basing their new strategic thrust partly upon their weakness in IT, the overall strategy is bound to fail.

That is why the simple but necessary addition of a "neutrals" line to the strengths and weaknesses analysis is vital, together with the absolute rule which follows.

When deciding the strategic thrust of a business, it must never be in any way dependent upon turning around a weakness in the organization's skills base. At best, it can include one neutral skill and then only if a credible plan to rapidly turn that neutral into a strength has been prepared and the resources necessary to achieve it voted into action.

This simple but vital rule has saved the strategies of many companies. The weaknesses of most organizations do not arise overnight. They develop because the organization has always neglected a particular area or just never managed to understand that subject. We mentioned IT above, but there are many other areas that some companies get wrong continuously. Some never master the art of selling. Their products may be so good they sell themselves. But if the company had selling skills, it could be twice as big. Other firms always lag behind in research and development (R&D). They

> *Weaknesses are endemic in most organizations and they are very difficult to change into strengths.*

copy other businesses when they issue new models or technological improvements, but they are never the first. For many years the Japanese thrived by copying any innovation developed in the USA or the UK.

Weaknesses are endemic in most organizations and they are very difficult to change into strengths. Indeed, the best that a business should hope for is to turn its weakness into a neutral. Even then it may take a considerable period of time. Similarly, it is possible to turn a neutral into a strength but, again, only with great effort and a considerable amount of time and, often, capital.

The implication of this rule is that a strategy can only succeed if it is largely based upon the recognized, real strengths of the business. When it is based upon a weakness it is highly likely to fail. Even when based upon a neutral, there should be a realistic plan in place to turn that neutral into a strength.

Turning around weaknesses and neutrals

Most businesses underestimate how difficult it is to improve weaknesses and neutrals. Managers do not just ignore the weaknesses. Usually they are aware of them and they often put major resources into improving them. However, there appears to be a *psychological* effect which results from putting heavy resources into turning around a weakness. Once an executive has committed the resources, it becomes increasingly more difficult to recognize when all the effort has had no effect.

This makes it even harder to grapple with the problem. Subordinates begin to "rearrange the truth" so their leader does not discover how badly the turnaround is going. Facts get distorted and soon the organization loses track of where it is. Executives then start taking decisions based on false data and the organization's really serious problems begin. One corporate client who sought my advice spends millions of dollars every year investigating customer attitudes toward its somewhat mediocre service. When the results are particularly poor in any one month, the senior executives actually give false data to the chairman, rather than show him the worst results. Of course, this also tells us something about this chairman, who obviously exudes more fear than is useful, if he really wishes to obtain honest information from his people.

It takes a long time to make a difference

Another equally important reason not to try to incorporate weaknesses as a key aspect of a strategic objective is that managers often underestimate how long it takes to turn a problem around. Most problems take a long time to develop. It is unwise to believe it will not take an equally long time to cure. Often a manager gets moved on to another area of responsibility before the cure is effected. The problem then goes back downhill to where it began. Another cause of failure in turning around important weaknesses is that they are culturally based. Unless the culture is changed, the problem will not be solved.

For example, if we continue the IT example started above. The first thing most organizations do to change this weakness is to appoint an IT director. He, in turn, will persuade the CEO to put a computer terminal on his desk to show the others that he cares about IT. However, almost nothing the IT director does will persuade the CEO to switch on his terminal, and that is what the CEO's subordinates will notice in the sense of cultural example. They will think that IT is still not important and, therefore, not worth taking trouble to learn to use themselves.

Internal change should be at the rate of change of the external environment

Some weaknesses are only perceptions. This may have often been the case with IT discussed above. IT has been developing at an astonishing rate for 40 years. The rate of growth has left everybody not intimately involved in the industry feeling that they are out of date every time they invest in any computer hardware or software. Thus, organizations always felt that they were missing opportunities that may never have been real for their industry anyway.

If leaders are to make rational judgments about their organization's weaknesses, they must keep an eye on the external rate of change. Most businesses now have the kind of IT which would have looked highly advanced just ten years ago. It often does simple bookkeeping, accounting, and billing functions which used to need many more people than now. Perhaps that is the most IT ever promised. They just had to wait a few years. Perhaps IT was never such a weakness in their businesses at all! The same applies to many other aspects of the internal SNW appraisal.

Your greatest strengths could be the source of your worst weaknesses

Although we have emphasized the difficulties of turning weaknesses into, at best, neutrals, the same does not apply to strengths. There is no reciprocal relationship. Thus, although you cannot turn weaknesses into strengths rapidly you can certainly turn strengths into weaknesses with great ease, in almost no time at all.

L'Oréal, a French-owned multinational which is a leader in beauty care and treatment industries, has a major strength in its ability to sell, through its sophisticated sales force. It is highly regarded by hair and beauty salons because it invests a higher percentage of its revenue in research and development than most of its competitors in the industry. Consequently, when L'Oréal salespeople announce a new breakthrough treatment, staff in hair and beauty salons (where L'Oréal first tries out most of its innovative products) buy large quantities on the strength of L'Oréal's previous excellent performance in making innovations in the industry. Occasionally L'Oréal gets it wrong, i.e. by marketing a product that just does not take as much hold of the public imagination as it estimated. On those occasions it would be easy for L'Oréal's strength to turn into a weakness with salons finding themselves loaded with bad stock that is unlikely to sell.

L'Oréal's reputation would be destroyed and its selling strength would have caused a weakness. L'Oréal is aware of this danger. It has a built-in safety device whereby the marketing department always controls the sales teams. If the marketing department recognizes that a mistake has been made because the sales to the public are not matching the promises of the salespeople to the retailers, then all stocks are automatically withdrawn and credited to their customers' accounts.

Choose internal strengths that are enduringly useful rather than ephemeral

It is important to work on strengths, neutrals, and weaknesses that are enduringly important and not ephemeral and merely fashionable. For example, continuously training staff to maintain high levels of customer service and responsiveness is more important than changing the corporate logo or staff uniforms to add a fashionable gloss to staff appearance. The same applies to other ephemeral fashions.

It was fashionable, in the mid-1990s, to "reengineer" businesses. This "reengineering product" was being sold by many leading consultancy firms. It could be a fad and may pass when the problems reengineering creates are more clearly perceived. Many companies are joining in this fashion, accepting and believing they have a weakness in terms of excess management layers. The 1990s have seen recession everywhere in the world at some time. At such times it is demonstrable that there will be apparently too many people in the company. But is reengineering the business at a time when everybody is feeling uncertain well advised? Many businesses are doing it

> *It is important to work on strengths, neutrals, and weaknesses that are enduringly important and not ephemeral and merely fashionable.*

because it is the fashion and reengineering seems to reduce costs in the medium term. However, the scar tissue of reengineering will exert its cultural effect long after the benefits from cost savings have disappeared. Certainly there may be some current value in the cost benefits – but the cost disadvantages of the loss of knowledge and loyalty from the human resource base of the business, are incalculable.

Communications is another constant problem in most organizations. All management questionnaires find communications are deemed insufficient in organizations; a manager can rarely give just the right amount of information to everybody. Different people have different needs whether it is to carry out their role for the organization or based upon their personal preference for more data. Communications also have a habit of becoming distorted as they travel up and down the hierarchy – or even along the ranks (the "Chinese Whispers" syndrome).

The best advice on solving organizational weaknesses is to carefully decide which of the trends is long term rather than temporary. It is not worth spending valuable human resource time turning around temporarily unfashionable or dysfunctional parts of the business.

Not science but good quality checklists

Business leaders find it difficult to find time to come to seminars and listen to lectures by learned academics because they are frequently "people in a hurry." What they often want is not a lecture but *solutions to problems*. They are prepared, if necessary, to listen to the whole seminar. But what they really want is simple "how to do it" advice on application of the theory.

Many of us have seen advertisements offering guaranteed winning formulae for football pools and lotteries or, even more ludicrous, advice on how to beat the bookmakers' odds on horse races. Few of us would be foolish enough to fall for this sales pitch. Business managers, however, want to believe academics, especially when they tell them "the answers."

Real business life cannot be subjected to the same scientific study that provides revelation in more developed sciences such as biology or mathematics. Human beings involved in business do not conform to scientifically predictable patterns. The science of business management is in its infancy. We will only know how infantile in a hundred years or so when somebody looks back and properly evaluates the foolishness of what today passes for business science.

> **Human beings involved in business do not conform to scientifically predictable patterns.**

If there is little science, what have all the academics been doing for the past 50 years? Well, they have not been wasting their time. In order to prepare their statistical analyses, they have had to gather data. The great benefit of collecting data is that they had to think about what data would be relevant to each subject. Therein lies the great benefit of their work. The relevant sets of data collected for analysis provide excellent *checklists*. These checklists can be used by business managers to ensure that they do not make mistakes when they think about their business. The audit sheets provided in this book are an example of just that – simple, comprehensive checklists which are intended to ensure that no important subject gets overlooked as you put your strategy together.

The checklist for strengths, neutrals, and weaknesses analysis

1 Accounting skills (financial)

This refers to the skills with which the accounting and financial managers of the business manipulate money, credit, loans, equity, debt, bonds, and all the instruments of financial management of the company. Skillful manipulation of the various means through which the organization raises and handles money can make huge additions to profitability or vulnerability. How well does the finance director conduct relationships with the company auditors, bankers, debenture holders, preference shareholders, other financial institutions, merchant bankers, or the stock exchange? Does he know where to get finance when it is needed? Does he understand how to link the results of the business with its strategic development, thereby keeping the institutional backers confident in the future?

2 Accounting skills (management)

Does the accounting function of the organization merely collect data or actively provide information to managers to help them manage the business better? Is the data it collects accurate? Is there a flexible accounting system which means that the leadership is able to run the business in the best way for the needs of the market?

In the cable industry it has been demonstrated that clients who opt to pay their monthly accounts by direct debit from their bank accounts are far less likely to switch to another supplier of telephony or entertainment than others. Furthermore, this form of payment is less costly to collect and more sure of collection than other systems. With information like that, it becomes important to assess what discount it is worth giving to customers who opt for direct debit, to ensure good overall customer management.

BT has, for many years, collected the subscription part of its income three months in advance. It does not take long to calculate the value of such an immense "loan" of three months free credit to BT from the subscription income from 25 million customers.

One company I have worked with completed its strategic analysis and decided that it would be in the best interests of the company to change from running its international businesses with a country structure to a structure based on market sectors, in order to match the increasing global approach of its customers. The state of its management accounting department was so ill-organized that the company was unable to install its preferred strategy because the accountants just could not supply the accounts in the required form. Consequently the company had to put back its strategic intentions and structure change for two years until the accountants could organize the changes. In the meantime, its global competitors were grabbing business and its opportunities were disappearing fast.

Another company I worked with had an accounting department which was so devious in its capacity to move revenue and profits around the businesses to maximize the company's avoidance of tax, that even the public limited company (plc) board directors could not recognize their own division's results when they emerged from the accounting department. The result of this was that the directors could never manage the corporation strategically from year to year because they were never really sure what was the true state of affairs in any of its businesses!

---

3 Access to finance

This may be confused with financial accounting skills. This category simply refers to whether the company is able to raise the necessary working capital to finance all its growth plans. Equally, if the company needs to carry out a substantial takeover of a competitor is there access to sufficient finance to complete the deal? These are the considerations of this category.

4 Business or divisional strategies

Divisional strategies in isolation are of little benefit and can be positively harmful if they happen to contradict the corporate strategy. The objective here is to see whether the separate divisions or businesses have their own strategies and, if they do, how well do they fit under the umbrella of the corporate strategy? Have the strategies been communicated to all relevant parties?

5 Corporate strategy

The judgment to be applied here is not just whether the organization has a corporate strategy but whether it is known and understood throughout the organization. A strategy which has not been communicated is barely more useful than no strategy at all.

It is necessary to differentiate between a strategy for the whole corporation and the category above, which refers to the strategy for each of the businesses.

Corporate strategy also refers to the "acceptability" of the strategy with the institutional and other investors. If it isn't credible to them, it probably isn't acceptable to the non-strategist, either. It is therefore probably not worth implementing because the institutions will withdraw their patronage. For example, Tomkins plc, a UK based conglomerate, has been told by its institutional investors that they don't believe in conglomerates any more. Greg Hutchings, its boss, keeps telling them that his diverse businesses are counter-cyclical to each other and that their good management makes the difference. Unfortunately, for him, they can vote with their shareholdings. They have chosen to hold the minimum, thus keeping Tomkins plc at a low value for its sector. Mr Hutchings has now announced that he may break the company into constituent parts to increase the value of the whole for the shareholders. This move should enable Tomkins plc to get back into the driving seat and start adding value again for its owners.

6 Cost structure of the business

Different businesses within the same industry can have different cost structures. These may be the consequences of the history of the organization, or a direct result of strategic practices. For example, did the founders buy business properties outright which are in the books at the original costs, and which carry no or low annual costs? Or does the organization rent all its property at current prices which may impose higher variable annual running costs upon the business than the competitor in the former situation?

Many cost structure differences may be the consequences of accounting policies. Does the organization write off capital costs over the true life of the capital or the fastest time permitted under the relevant tax laws? How does it value semimanufactured stock? Are there reserves against bad debts or are they an annual hazard? An accumulation of small past decisions and policies on subjects such as these may mean that two competing organizations in the same industry have substantially different cost bases. This may prove to be a major liability for an organization with a high cost base in the market. For example, for a business which writes five year contracts with its clients, the property charge policy could make an enormous difference to its contract costings and thus the contract price to the customer. A salesman could consistently lose out on bids for new business because the cost structure of the business is managed differently from that of its competitors.

7 Distribution network

A firm's distribution network can be strategically important in giving it the ability to control entry into its industry by competitors. For example, Coca-Cola has an immensely strong grip upon the distribution network of the soft drinks industry throughout the USA. When Cadbury-Schweppes, a UK soft drinks company, wanted to enter that market it was unable to make any headway for many years. Finally it gained some penetration by agreeing to allow Coca-Cola equal access into the UK through the joint marketing company they formed to distribute both Coca-Cola and Schweppes products in the UK.

8 Entry barriers

How difficult is it to enter the industry or business the organization is involved in? For example, is the business *capital intensive* or is it possible to enter the industry with low start-up costs? It is hard to imagine how to start up a small scale car manufacturing plant. So the initial start-up costs would be an effective entry barrier. On the other hand, it may be relatively easy to start a manufacturing line of washing powder. Many of these products, however, have strong brand loyalty. In the case of powder detergents, although it may be easy to enter the industry from the cost of manufacturing angle, it would take large amounts of capital to build the high level of brand loyalty already enjoyed by the two giants which dominate this world industry, Procter & Gamble, and its rival Unilever. Incidentally, the next entry barrier for powder detergents is to capture space on the shelves the incumbents control because their brands are already bestsellers. A new entrant would have to prove to a retailer that its product would guarantee equal or better profit per square foot of space to have any chance of getting onto the shelves at all.

9 Exit barriers

This category is the opposite of the previous one. How hard is it to leave the industry or industries the organization is in? For example, the longer a company has been in business in most countries which have laws protecting employees' rights, the more expensive it will be to remove staff when closing down. Other prime exit barriers are long leases or freeholds of property which cannot be used for anything other than the occupants' use. This may lock an organization into a loss-making business where, in spite of the losses, it is still cheaper to stay in and lose money rather than pay the cost of exit.

However, a poor assessment of long-term strategic weakness and apparent high exit barriers can sometimes lead to false economies. One corporation I worked with reckoned the exit cost from its parcels business was £25 million. It calculated that it was better off staying in the business and trying to get it right. Over the course of the eight years that I observed the situation, it endured another £40 million in trading losses. Even worse, it continued to send its best managers to try to solve the problem. When they failed it blamed them and asked them to leave, forgetting that it was the business which was no good and not the executives trying to turn it around. It became known as a managers' graveyard. Ultimately, the cost of the financial losses, plus the excellent executives lost to the corporation via this catastrophe area, was much higher than the original cost of exit eight years earlier.

10 Information technology skills

We have discussed IT extensively enough elsewhere in this chapter for the reader to have sufficient criteria to judge whether IT is a strength, a neutral, or a weakness.

11 Lateral communications

This refers to communications at any level in the hierarchy between people on the same level. One often finds managers who are happy to communicate with their superiors or with their subordinates but who are, conversely, highly reluctant to communicate with each other. Sometimes they do not realize that their information is relevant to their colleagues' work. However, more often it is because they see members of their peer group as rivals for their next promotion. Withholding information is a source of power and control. They believe it will ensure that they keep the upper hand.

12 Leader's ability

This is one of the hardest to judge. After all, the leader is meant to manage the longer time horizons of the business and can, therefore, only be properly judged over, say, a three to five-year term. The problem is that one can only find out how well a leader really led the organization long after he has left it.

However, this does not mean one is unable to make judgments, merely that it is difficult. A good leader will inspire confidence that he is getting it right. People will understand what he is trying to do. They will feel confident that the company is going places and those places are worth going to.

One should not confuse charisma or personality with leadership skills or character. Sometimes leaders have charisma or they develop it. But it is not a requirement of leadership. Sometimes it actually gets in the way because the people paid to make judgments about the CEO, such as the non-executive directors or the chairman, may be prevented from seeing what an appalling job is being done by the leader because he is able to confuse their judgment by charismatic behavior which dazzles, but ultimately achieves nothing.

One organization I worked with (a UK plc), has regularly changed its strategy every year to explain why last year's results are below par and the new strategy will resolve the problems and set the company in a new, more successful direction. The chairman has great charisma and presentation skills. It is astonishing that the City of London analysts have allowed him to pull the wool over their eyes for the 20 years he has been pulling this stunt. Every year I watch him do it again. But he is never asked the hard questions like: "Why did the strategy of last year and the previous year fail, when it was explained as rationally and charismatically as this one?" Or, "Why should anybody believe him this year?" But he gets away with it on pure personality. Unfortunately, underlying this abuse of charisma is a history of his making hundreds of people redundant each time another tactic fails. The chairman himself is a wealthy man after so many years at the top (and he inherited his shareholding from his father anyway).

13 Leadership skills in general

Aside from the leader's skills, do the managers in general demonstrate high quality leadership skills in the business and with their teams or are they merely representatives carrying out instructions and filling in forms?

14 Loyalty of the workforce

How loyal are the employees? Would they rather work for your company than any other in the industry? What premium in salary would it take for your rivals or your customers to headhunt your best managers? How many senior executives have you lost in the past year and did they go to work for your most powerful competitors or merely exit the industry? Did you want them to go? Would you have preferred that they stayed? Are you telling yourself the truth or just rationalizing their departure with phrases such as, "I'm not sorry to see them go"?

15 Management ability

A similar set of questions applies to the management. Do the managers really control their parts of the business or do they merely obey instructions. Do they know how to get results from their people and do they understand delegation? Do they get things done through their team or do they really do most of the work themselves? On the other hand, are they so busy managing that they have forgotten how to get their hands dirty in a crisis?

One measure of the quality of management is given by examination of the company's management development programs. Is management training evolutionary, developing a manager over the whole course of his career? Or is it a one-off skills program? Are managers continuously retrained even if they have not been recently promoted? Does management training stop at senior levels with the underlying assumption that they probably know it all by the time they achieve senior levels in the organization?

16 Manufacturing skills

Does the business know how to make the things it claims to be able to provide in a timely manner with high quality? One is reminded of the legendary "quality story" of the UK firm that had decided to out-source the manufacture of one of the components which it had previously made in-house. The UK firm had much lower standards of quality than the Japanese supplier which it asked to supply some components. The UK firm set what it considered to be a stringent quality standard of three faulty components per thousand delivered. The components were delivered in two boxes, with an accompanying letter. The letter said, "Please find the 1000 components ordered. In the second, smaller box you will find the three faulty components you also requested."

17 Marketing skills

This refers to the general marketing skills of the company. Does it have relevant data about its markets? Does it use all the tools of advertising, promotion, and PR fully? Does the marketing department control sales (the way it should) or vice versa? Does the company handle its product life cycles actively or passively? Does the marketing department collect data about competitors, and their products, and does it disseminate the information to the relevant managers? Does it conduct focus groups and continuously provide data to improve the product or services of the business to increase market penetration?

If too many of the answers to these questions are negative, then you need to decide whether the organization's marketing skills are neutral or a weakness.

18 Organizational structure

This refers to the way the company is organized. Does the organization structure get in the way of the implementation of strategy or help it? Are customers confused because they receive visits from more than one salesperson for different parts of the product range? Does the structure facilitate marketing and selling? Is it easy to communicate with other members of the firm? Are staff easily promoted between divisions, businesses, and departments as their careers develop, so they can gain wide experience, or does the structure get in the way?

These questions and their answers will indicate whether this category is one of the better or worse aspects of the organization's internal environment.

19 Products

The portfolio of products or services the organization offers to its customers is a key strength or weakness. Is it comprehensive? Is there a vital ingredient or product that is controlled by a competitor? Does the organization's range compare favorably with those of competitors? Where does the customer shop first? Considerations such as these will define the quality of the organization's service or product range.

20 Quality of brands

Although this category generally applies more to retail businesses, many industrial businesses have important brands that add value to their products, provide barriers against imitation and help maintain price differentials against rival products and services. The value of brands has received increasing attention from the accounting profession in recent years. The costs of building a brand to rival a competitor's established product brand name is often sufficient to deter strategic leaders from competing at all.

21 Quality of staff

The quality of staff plays an important part in the potential strategic opportunities facing the organization as well as the choice of routes an organization might adopt to get there. The quality of staff will be dependent upon past human resource policies, the amount of investment in training and developing people in the past and the general attitude of management to people (usually with guidance on style from the leadership of the organization). In the course of time all these elements become a force for strength or weakness.

In addition, the type of workforce may be dictated by the industry itself. For example, in the information technology software industry, the workforce tends to be well educated, sophisticated, and relatively independent-minded. The methods needed to manage a sophisticated workforce such as this will be substantially different from the strategic style that would be effective in an industry with more manually skilled employees.

22 Reputation in the marketplace

A company's reputation is vitally important to all aspects of its business. A company often needs a good reputation to achieve its objectives. It can also be frustrated in achieving its purposes if it has a poor reputation. Some acquire a good reputation for some aspects of their business, while retaining a poor reputation concerning other parts. For example, some years ago, BT had a poor reputation for the quality of its basic telephony service. At the same time market research demonstrated that its reputation for the standard of its products (such as telephones and switching systems) was high.

A good reputation has many benefits and a bad reputation has more power for ill than first appraisal might show. For example, when the organization's reputation is sound, customers make strong, good assumptions about your products and give the organization the benefit of the doubt when things go wrong. On the other hand, a company with a poor reputation can do nothing right in the eyes of its public.

Another important measure of reputation is the quality of people the company attracts. For example, does your company get the best pick of the graduates from universities or other sources of labor? Does it have to pay in the upper quartiles by industry norms or can it pay mid-level salaries and still attract and retain the best people?

Is your company reputed for excellence or mediocrity? Do the employees feel they have to apologize for where they work or, even worse, avoid mentioning the company's name in polite society? These are the measures of reputation.

One executive I was training told me how he had been sent, as chief executive, to sort out a catastrophic situation in his company's Australian subsidiary. The previous chief executive had fiddled the books for three years before being caught and dismissed. The customers were up in arms because the quality of product had deteriorated and they were suing the company for failure to meet contractual obligations – quite justifiably.

When the new boss arrived in Australia he decided that the only thing to do was to face the music and meet all the complainants to sort out the problems. He further decided that he had better meet all the non-customers and find out what they thought about the company. He discovered that every important buyer in the industry was prepared to meet him to tell him what an appalling condition they thought the company had been allowed to descend into. They were even ready to give the company new business, eventually, if he could turn things around. The story demonstrates the power of reputation. Even though the recent past had been dreadful the customers were still willing to talk, and eventually, forgive and forget.

---

23 Relationship with government or regulator

Some organizations work hard to ensure they have relationships with politicians or, sometimes more influentially, with the advisers who guide legislators on policy and legislation. This can be an important source of profitability and control in an industry. The ability to influence standards and rules governing an industry can be a powerful tool to prevent competition or control the costs of entry into the business.

This explains why so many new industries, after a few years' trading, set up an industry federation which then tries to persuade the government to pass legislation to ensure standards in the industry. In fact, what it really does is to pull up a drawbridge behind those safely ensconced in the industry and ensure that they can divide up the profit spoils amongst themselves. These standards act as a deterrent and barrier against potential entrants into the industry.

The same considerations apply to many privatized enterprises which are controlled by a regulator who largely replaces the role previously fulfilled by a Cabinet Minister. In the UK, British Gas (the corporation controlling the supply of all gas in the UK) was privatized with a virtual monopoly of its industry. Its customers received poor service and its relations with its regulator deteriorated into a virtual slanging match. Subsequently, it lost its monopoly and, probably, its long-term profitability.

24 Relationship with suppliers

Old-fashioned views about relationships with suppliers have traditionally been that they were servants to the customer and were broadly obliged to do what the customer wanted. As many more industries have become oligopolies and the choices of suppliers diminish, it becomes more vitally important to have an excellent relationship with suppliers based on mutual respect and self-interest.

For example, is your organization the supplier's preferred customer? Is the supplier willing to fund or enter a joint venture to assist with research and development in your organization? Would you be the first customer the supplier would think of if he received an inquiry for your product and was asked for a recommendation?

25 Selling skills

How effective is the sales force? Can they sell the maximum quantity or are they content to merely meet non-stretching targets? A sales force should be proactive, looking for market opportunities and continuously nagging its managers to bring out new designs and informing them of the demand for new products.

One industry which has some of the best sales forces in the world is the pharmaceutical industry. This strength has led the industry into an interesting strategic dilemma. They have been so successful in selling drugs to doctors and hospitals throughout the 1980s that they have created, in the 1990s, a swell of public opinion which has decided they are too successful and profitable. This, in turn, is handing political power caused by adverse public opinion, to politicians who can then change the rules governing patent protection. This may lead to decreases in profitability for the pharmaceutical majors – a clear case of a strength being used so indiscriminately that it becomes a weakness.

26 Vertical communication

Communications is probably the one subject that almost every group of leaders and managers believes it does less effectively than it wishes. Similarly, it is the one common complaint from all workforces that they do not receive enough feedback and information about the parts of the organization they know little about.

Both sides are probably wrong to some extent for there must be limits to how much information is sent up and down the line, if only to prevent excess information leading to less rather than more actual communication.

However, there are objective measures available and these can be used to measure whether vertical communication is effective or not. Most organizations that are better at this tend to use *employee attitude surveys* on a regular basis. These can give sophisticated feedback on how much information employees are actually receiving as well as how they feel about their managers and leaders. Such surveys are best used on a regular basis and monitored carefully for changes in key measures.

A note on the profitability of industries

Some industries have chronic excess supply problems. This may be due to particularly low barriers to entry, attracting excess supply to the industry as soon as some firm in the industry reports higher than usual profits for the year. It could be due to having "lumpy" technology, meaning that the economies of production in that industry are large. For example, one cannot build a small steel manufacturing plant. If a firm in such an industry builds just one major new plant the whole industry could be tipped into oversupply from marginal undersupply. Such a condition will keep a tight cap on potential profits and possibly push the industry into chronic losses.

If you decide your business is in an industry plagued by this "supply lumpiness" problem, when you come to make your decisions about the strategy, you may wish to consider whether you have any opportunities to move your business into more profitable sectors, either upstream (closer to manufacture) or downstream (closer to retail). You may decide you want to exit the industry completely, over time.

The problem of objectivity

The hardest aspect of conducting an audit of the organization's internal strengths, neutrals, and weaknesses is the difficulty of retaining objective judgment. This is even harder when assessing areas of known weakness where the organization has made a special effort to improve. One must accept that there can be no absolute objectivity. All judgments in the areas we are examining are, of necessity, subjective. However, when making such judgments the value of belief can actually impede progress rather than act as a catalyst for positive good.

Belief in the organization and in the results one is aiming for is usually a key way to achieve the extra edge over competitors. However, when it comes to assessing the SNW situation of the business, belief must be set aside in favor of the most absolute objectivity you can manage. If a category is bad, admit it and face the change implications! Ruthless honesty is the key to achieving an accurate SNW analysis. After all, the only person you can fool in this internal analysis is yourself!

Additional reading for this chapter

G. Hamel and C. K. Pralahad, *Competing for the Future*, Harvard Business School Press, Boston, 1994

C. Handy, *Understanding Organizations* (4th edn), Penguin, London, 1993

J. Hunt, *Managing People at Work*, Pan, London, 1981

J. Kay, *Foundations of Corporate Success*, Oxford University Press, Oxford, 1993

C. Levicki, *The Leadership Gene*, Financial Times Pitman Publishing, London, 1998

T. J. Peters and R. H. Waterman, *In Search of Excellence*, Harper & Row, New York, 1982

S. Slatter, *Corporate Recovery*, Penguin, Middlesex, 1984

STRENGTHS, NEUTRALS, AND
WEAKNESSES WORKOUT

Check each of the following categories in terms of it being a strength, neutral, or a weakness.

Sometimes it helps to allocate a number from 1 to 5 indicating high (5), medium (3), or low (1). Thus, a Neutral with a 5 on it would be very close to a Strength with a 1 on the same category.

Organization function	Strength	Neutral	Weakness
Accounting skills (financial)	❏	❏	❏
Accounting skills (management)	❏	❏	❏
Access to finance	❏	❏	❏
Business strategy	❏	❏	❏
Corporate strategy	❏	❏	❏
Cost structure of business	❏	❏	❏
Distribution network	❏	❏	❏
Divisional strategy	❏	❏	❏
Entry barriers	❏	❏	❏
Exit barriers	❏	❏	❏
Information technology	❏	❏	❏
Innovation (turning research into products)	❏	❏	❏
Lateral communication	❏	❏	❏
Leader's ability	❏	❏	❏
Leadership in general	❏	❏	❏
Loyalty of workforce	❏	❏	❏
Management ability	❏	❏	❏
Manufacturing skills	❏	❏	❏
Marketing skills	❏	❏	❏
Organization structure	❏	❏	❏
Products	❏	❏	❏
Quality of brands	❏	❏	❏
Quality of staff	❏	❏	❏

STRENGTHS, NEUTRALS, AND WEAKNESSES

WORKOUT (cont)

Organization function	Strength	Neutral	Weakness
Reputation in market	❑	❑	❑
Reputation as employer	❑	❑	❑
Relationship with government	❑	❑	❑
Relationship with regulator	❑	❑	❑
Relationship with trade unions	❑	❑	❑
Relationships with suppliers	❑	❑	❑
Research and development	❑	❑	❑
Services	❑	❑	❑
Selling skills	❑	❑	❑
Technical engineering skills	❑	❑	❑
Personnel administration	❑,	❑	❑
Vertical communication	❑	❑	❑

Additional categories
(*Relevant to your particular business*)

	Strength	Neutral	Weakness
_____	❑	❑	❑
_____	❑	❑	❑
_____	❑	❑	❑

SUMMARY OF SNW WORKOUT

Select the top four strengths, neutrals, and weaknesses from your analysis on the previous audit pages and set them out below with a brief note on how you might use, neutralize, or improve the effects of each on the success of the organization's mission.

The strengths

1 _____

2 _____

3 _____

4 _____

The neutrals

1 _____

2 _____

3 _____

4 _____

The weaknesses

1 _____

2 _____

3 _____

4 _____

Organizational Culture
Or How Do We Really Do Things Around Here?

Culture is positive and difficult to change

History and its effect upon the present

How to notice mental and physical environments

How past and present leaders affect the way people do things

Technology affects culture too

Myths, legends, stories, anecdotes, and their effect upon the organization

Possibly the most important feature of culture is that it is a measure of the state of things as they currently exist, rather than as one would like them to be.

"There was, of course, a catch.
'Catch-22' inquired Yossarian.
'It's your fault' Yossarian argued, 'for raising the number
of missions.'
'No, it's your fault for refusing to fly them,' Colonel Korn
retorted."

From *Catch-22*, by Joseph Heller

Culture – what is it?

The *culture of any organization* is the corporate equivalent of the personal psychology of a human being. An individual's psychological makeup defines his personality, how he behaves, what he looks like to others and what he does and does not do in relation to any set of circumstances. The culture of an organization operates in a similar way and defines the kind of things the organization can and cannot do. It becomes a predictor of what changes are likely to succeed and those which will not. The culture of an organization defines most aspects of its potential in the same way that an individual's psychology largely controls his successes and failures in life.

Culture is a strong force because it is a combination of history, trauma, and habit. The longer the history of the organization, the more habits will have evolved, and the less easy it will be to change those habits. Often habitual behavior becomes entirely disconnected from the reasons for the behavior. For example, the waiter in a restaurant who carefully brushes the bread crumbs from the table before serving dessert. There may or may not be crumbs to clear, but he will brush the table even if there are none.

More substantially distorting, habitual behaviors often occur in factories and offices when new systems arrive but behavior does not change to match them.

A classic example occurred in a car battery manufacturing business which rebuilt its stockroom. The scrapped stockroom had been circular in shape. The stockkeepers used a round carousel holding stock cards to keep track of where the stock was laid out in the circular room. Unfortunately, when they changed to a rectangular stockroom they failed to change the carousel. Within months the round carousel had lost track of many thousands of batteries in the square corners of the new stockroom. Some years later the carousel system was still in operation, but the problem had worsened. When the stockroom clerks realized that batteries were being lost from the stockkeeping system they decided to appropriate them to sell for their personal gain. That is how the company acquired a theft problem too!

The longer an organization has been in existence, the greater the trauma it will have suffered. Trauma leaves indelible scars below the surface of the business. They disappear from sight, but this does not prevent the scars from having an effect.

For example, British Gas, a UK utility, has a long tradition of arrogance and lack of flexibility. It has found it almost impossible to change its culture and become customer responsive. Consequently, it lost shareholder value as it ruined its relationship with its UK regulator, as a direct result of its inability to achieve a flexible working relationship.

The culture audit looks at "What is" – culture change looks at "What should be"

Possibly the most important feature of culture is that it is a measure of *the state of things as they currently exist,* rather than as one would like them to be. A most powerful culture exercise is to get the senior managers of a company to conduct a culture audit of their present culture – *"the way we do things around here now."* Then get them to imagine themselves in their company five years hence and conduct a culture audit of the future company and *"how we ought to be doing things around here in five years' time"*

What will be the important historical events in the future? What will the physical and mental environment be like then? Who will be the "past leaders" in the future and what lessons will they have left behind? Who will be the

> *Culture is a measure of the state of things as they currently exist, rather than as one would like them to be.*

present leaders in the future? What technologies will be prevalent in the future company? Most importantly, what myths, stories, and legends will they have left behind to guide people in the future about *how we do things around here now?* It is a powerful exercise and demonstrates effectively the paths of behavior change that will be necessary in the company, if the strategic future is to be attained.

Components of the culture audit

1 History

The key cultural lessons to be learned from the history of the organization require the strategist to examine important historical events and decide which of those events have left patterns which still affect the way people in the organization do things. Sometimes history leaves traditions that people continue to live up to but which prevent them from doing things in more fashionable or effective ways.

In general, the longer the history of the organization, the more important its effect; the longer people within it have been doing things in a particular way, the more ingrained the behavior becomes. The cultural effect gets stronger as behaviors become removed from the reasons for the action. In England, for example, some organizations still retain a "char lady" who goes around the building mornings and afternoons dispensing tea and coffee. There are adequate mechanized ways of providing the same service to staff from beverage dispensers. People in organizations which retain the older style method often insist that the lady is part of the furniture and that they would never replace her. She is part and parcel of the culture, for good and bad; she contributes to "the way we do things around here" in that organization.

Another important way that history can affect an organization's culture is through major historical events that cause "scarring" in the collective memory of the organization. Such events may be the burning down of an important depot or some time when the organization nearly ran out of cash.

Particular events create historical scar tissue, and ingrained habits come from carrying out processes in a regular way so that one almost does not have to think about the process any more. Thus, habitual behavior and history create a mental environment which affect the way things are done in the organization.

The effects of history: British Gas

When studying background material to conduct research on British Gas, I came across historical documents which outlined the policy of the original, nineteenth century, London Gas, Light and Coke Company. This document set out some appalling penalties meted out to employees for misdemeanors. Even taking account of the harsher attitudes of employers in the nineteenth century, this was a model of severity. Late arrival at work could result in the loss of the whole day's pay. Rudeness to an official would be punished by instant dismissal with no recourse to appeal.

Today, in the modern British Gas Corporation, the London region remains intransigent and its relations with the workforce have not improved much. How much of that scar tissue was formed by the original documents and hostility created by the medieval rules of the original London Gas, Light and Coke Company?

2 The mental environment of the organization

The mental environment is caused by the attitudes and management styles of managers in the organization. Thus, if they are autocratic, the mental environment will reflect this. If they are participative, their subordinates will mentally ingest this and mirror their behavior.

There may be more subtle mental atmospheres. Some organizations have an atmosphere of fear or dishonesty whereas others transmit honesty; some are open and welcoming to outsiders while others have a closed attitude. There is a natural intellectual ambience in some organizations (sometimes related to a high percentage of graduates among employees) which may contrast with a deliberate, vulgar stupidity in others. Some firms build in respect for everybody, within and outside the firm. Others see employees and customers as victims or bait. The insurance industry of the 1980s in the UK seems to have had an atmosphere of suspended ethics wherein it was difficult to openly ask about the moral tone of the way clients were being sold pension schemes which were against their interests.

The effects of mental atmosphere (1): IBM

IBM in the 1980s had an utterly closed outlook upon the world. IBMers knew they were excellent; the world cited them as the arch example of how an excellent company should be run, and they believed it themselves. They arrived at a state of increasing self-sufficiency. They even used their state-of-the-art internal electronic mail so they could talk to each other at any time (usually in preference to talking to outsiders).

The personnel of IBM were universally well educated and of a high caliber. They wore similar clothing. They understood each other and were comfortable with each other. It was a complete internal world and they needed no other. It was so internally complete that they failed to notice that the external world was moving on and no longer needed what IBM was offering.

Microsoft, Novell, Intel, and countless other computer hardware and software companies had seen the changes taking place in the real world and were invading the marketplace that had belonged traditionally to IBM for many years. The mental atmosphere had moved IBM too far away from market reality – and it almost cost IBM its economic life.

The effects of mental atmosphere (2): Scandinavian Airlines Services

Another example of the creation of a mental environment was the story of Scandinavian Airlines Services (SAS) in the 1980s. SAS acquired a new leader named Jan Carlson. He had a marketing background and believed in giving customers what they wanted. However, when he became the head of SAS, it was a typical government-controlled bureaucracy (the Scandinavian governments held equal shares in SAS).

Carlson soon realized that the customers' sense of satisfaction was not the same as the things which gave satisfaction to airline employees. Employees cared about having modem, high-technology airplanes. Carlson understood that customers cared about the comfort of the seating, getting to their destination on time and, for business people especially, getting a peaceful and untroubled ride.

Carlson knew he could not change everything at once. So he decided to focus on one area, punctuality, to help change the mental outlook of the business. He ran a campaign within and outside SAS, explaining that it would always try to get its travelers to their destinations on time.

He even installed a giant electronic wall chart in his office which told him what time every plane in SAS service was taking off. If a pilot was even a few minutes late on takeoff, Carlson would be on the phone just a few moments later, talking to the pilot, asking him whether he thought he would be able to make up the late takeoff time during the flight.

You can imagine the mental climate that he created as he harried and nagged his people, both on the ground or in the air, to be on time. Within two years of Carlson taking over at SAS, it moved from being almost unknown to the average airline user, to being voted International Airline of the Year.

3 Past leaders

Past leaders can leave a style and pace of doing things which lives on many years after they have left the organization. It is a useful exercise to ask managers what they will be remembered for in ten years' time when they are long gone from their current roles in their organizations. Most will look blank faced and reply that they have not thought about it. They should. Either they will not be remembered at all (which, for some, might be a blessing), or they will be remembered for things they would prefer to be forgotten. Most managers who make a difference are remembered distinctly for two or three simple principles which they decide are important in the job they are doing at any time.

> **Most managers who make a difference are remembered distinctly for two or three simple principles which they decide are important in the job they are doing at any time.**

The behavioral effects of past leaders: Sir Don Ryder at Reed International

Reed Elsevier (which used to be called Reed International) transformed itself from a business involved almost entirely in the packaging industry to one involved almost exclusively in the publishing industry (see Chapter 2). The pattern for these large-scale maneuvers was set by Sir Don Ryder who had been a leader in the organization many years before.

Sir Don had a reputation for turning up outside large factories all over the country and confronting their owners with "an offer they couldn't refuse." He rarely received an immediate "yes," but equally, he rarely departed without buying the factory he had set his heart on bringing into Reed International ownership, even if he had to pay too much – another cultural tradition that Reed Elsevier appears to have inherited.

Sir Don always retained a style of large-scale buying and selling. He loved massive organizational transformation in grand moves. This was the pattern of behavior he set in the organization. Decades later, the leaders of the 1990s were obeying the cultural imperatives set by the early leadership style of Sir Don Ryder when they left the packaging industry completely and entered the publishing industry.

4 Present leaders

The same considerations which apply to past leaders apply even more strongly to present leaders. Everything chairmen and chief executives do is studied by subordinates and frequently imitated. Leaders should always be aware of the effect of their style and manner, for they never know when they are starting a trend. They cannot help some mannerisms or idiosyncrasies of style but it is surprising what is copied: heavy drinking, swearing, kindness, or indifference are all styles that are easily imitated. Do they choose to be driven by a chauffeur, or do they drive themselves? (One well-known leader was famous among his directors for getting out of his Rolls-Royce and exchanging it for a Ford a few roads away from his office, believing that he was setting an example to the rest of the team. Actually they all knew what he was doing. What was the final effect?) Some leaders speak politely to subordinates, others are gruff and rude. Does the leader care about cash flow or merely encourage people to find profits in any crooked way possible? Any of these patterns will be picked up and imitated by managers throughout an organization.

The behavioral effects of current leaders: Dauphin Distribution

I was working once with a CEO in Pennsylvania. He was the leader of a food distribution company and he was showing me around his warehouses. As we walked around, I noticed he would stop every few feet and bend down and pretend to pick up a piece of paper or litter. When we arrived back in his office, I asked him why he had been picking up imaginary pieces of litter. His response was telling. I just like to keep reminding my people that in the food business we have to be obsessive about hygiene. They are so good that I rarely find any litter. But when I keep bending down like that – and I know they are watching me on the cameras in the office – they think I have really found something and they remain as obsessive as I am about hygiene!

A key question for the reader is whether there is a fundamental flaw in setting a desirable standard of hygiene by means of manipulative (and, therefore, undesirable) behavior.

Behavioral effects of current leaders: XYZ Engineering

The chief executive of a large engineering concern (called XYZ Engineering to disguise his identity) was a bright man who liked people and hated confrontation of any type. Sometimes he backed away from positions he really cared about because the people performing badly were too aggressive for him to confront with their inadequate performance. He and I had agreed that it was vitally important to get his people to agree to live by a fundamental principle that, when they made commitments to an operating budget, it would represent an absolute promise to deliver that budget.

That year, deliberately, he did not push them too hard on their budgets to ensure they were manifestly achievable. At the start of the year we ran a seminar for his senior executives where we achieved unanimous agreement with the senior executives that they wanted to conform to the principle of delivering promises on budgets. They also agreed to get their subordinates to deliver to them in accordance with the same principle. At the close of the seminar the chief executive made the following speech:

"I know I have promised to deliver £35.8 million profit to the chairman this year. However, you'll be pleased to know that I think the chairman only expects £25 million. The City analysts will even accept £20 million. So you'll understand why I'm not as worried as you might expect me to be about this year's poor results!"

No comment is needed as to the mistake he made. Within a few months every executive was behind on his budget promises and the chief executive had to issue a profits shortfall warning to the Stock Exchange. He was dismissed by his chairman a week later when the share price halved as a consequence of his announcement.

5 The physical environment

The physical surroundings of an organization can play as large a part in "the way people do things around here" as does the mental environment. Physical circumstances have an insidious effect upon people, for both good and ill. Sometimes the worst effects are caused by the contrast between the environment of different parts of the business. Frequently one finds that corporate head offices are housed in beautiful buildings with stylish furniture and luscious plants abounding. When one visits the manufacturing sites, where the real money is being earned for the company, one finds a contrasting element of squalor, neglect, or dinginess. Some HQ people argue that "the workers don't notice such things." Do you believe them? What effect do such contrasts really have upon workers? What should the policy of your organization be on such cultural factors?

Many factors contribute to the overall physical environment, e.g. whether the organization generally has computers on desks or whether people still use administration systems run by people, paper, and pencils.

One organization I worked with had installed a computerized system for logging clients' rentals of its equipment. Previously it had a card index system to log what equipment was being used and where. I asked one assistant to demonstrate the system to me. When she demonstrated the computer system to me, I noticed the numbers on the computer were all blank. I asked why. She explained that, although she had been ordered to do it, she really did not trust it – so she continued to fill in the card system. She did the minimum computer filing to satisfy her superiors who were very committed to making the computer system work. She admitted that she had been doing unpaid overtime because of all the extra work the computer was causing!

6 Technology and its effect on culture

The technology a firm employs can also play an important part in the development of its culture. What the firm does and how it does it, create habits of thought and behavior which eventually become entrenched. Does the production process need thought or can it be carried out automatically? Are the offices paper-based or do they use computers? Is the business high technology or low technology, giving a tradition of modern against more traditional modes of work? One thinks here of the difference between the quiet efficiency of, say, the electricity supply industry compared to the traditional ways of doing things represented by the coal industry; contrast that, again, to a software company like Microsoft with dedicated brainworkers quietly creating wealth at their work stations.

> **What the firm does and how it does it, create habits of thought and behavior which eventually become entrenched.**

Is the business involved in process or batch work? Joan Woodward, an Oxford University academic (see her study, *Industrial Organisation: Behaviour and Control*, Oxford University Press, London, 1970), carried out studies to see the effects of technology on businesses. She found important differences between batch and process technologies. What we are asserting here is that each of the subtle differences of technology has its own culture effect.

The effects of a change in technology

Some years ago the managing director of Berol, a company then specializing in the manufacture of felt tip pens, decided that it was missing large profit opportunities because it only supplied wholesale clients. He decided to change its distribution policy and supply direct to large retailers.

Unfortunately, the company did not quite foresee what a vast difference the change would make to the business and it nearly failed as a result. Prior to the change in distribution policy, it had been a process company. To supply its wholesalers it used to take scale decisions to manufacture (say) 10 million grey felt tip pens; then, 10 million red ones, and so on. These were supplied to wholesalers and the wholesalers had the worry of holding stock, making mixes of different colors, and satisfying their retail clients.

After the company decided to supply direct to retailers, a totally different situation suddenly applied. Retailers sell packs of mixed colors of felt tip pens in a highly seasonable pattern, with peaks at Christmas, Easter, and in the summer break. Furthermore, they do not like to hold excess stock at other times of the year. When Berol's new retail clients ran out of stock, they would telephone Berol and scream for more supplies and immediate delivery, and they did not want 1 million grey ones; they wanted 100 000 packs of ten mixed colors.

This completely changed the culture and profile of Berol's business. It could no longer just make production a function of the production manager's budget; it had to become an instrument of customers' demand patterns. Berol had to change its manufacturing away from a process system to a batch system to meet the demand for mixed color packs with seasonal peaks, rather than wholesale orders for single colors.

It may seem surprising that these matters were not all foreseen by the managers when they took their apparently simple decision to make a change in their distribution policy. But the traumatic changes were cultural rather than just procedural. Berol nearly went under as a consequence and was lucky to survive the decision.

7 Myths and legends within the organization

Myths and legends have an enormous effect upon the way people do things in organizations. They are used as exemplars to encourage the kind of behavior wanted in the organization. They guide people on what to do and how to do it.

Myths and legends differ from anecdotes and stories because their origins tend to be based more deeply in the distant past and they may bear less resemblance to actual events that may have taken place. They become twisted over time to form a shorthand summary of "the way things developed here" or "a warning lesson."

> **Myths and legends have an enormous effect upon the way people do things in organizations.**

The difficulty in using myths and legends is that, to a large extent, they have a life of their own and cannot be created. Thus, one may choose to emphasize some and de-emphasize others to stimulate an effect one desires.

The effects of myths and legends

A powerful myth used to have negative effects at BT. I once asked some senior managers at BT why they had so much trouble keeping their street pay phones working when there was no such problem for Nynex in New York.

"That's easy," they responded. "In New York the Mafia use street phones to communicate with each other to bypass the phone-tapping of the FBI. If anyone is caught vandalizing pay phones in New York, the Mafia would cut their hands off – so the vandals leave them alone."

The implication was that BT did not have the benefit of the Mafia in the UK to prevent phones from being vandalized. How could it be expected to keep its pay phones in working order?

Even senior managers allowed this myth to excuse them from trying to keep pay phones in working order. The problem was later sorted by an innovative young manager who refused to let the myth beat him. The pay phones are now working well and make good profits for the company.

8 Stories and anecdotes

The difference between myths and legends and the next category of culture variables – stories and anecdotes – is that the latter are based more on fact than are myths and legends. Usually, stories and anecdotes are more recent; they can be a more powerful cultural tool than myths and legends because they can be created by leaders to achieve particular and general purposes.

For example, to encourage customer care, a manager can choose to do something very special for a customer that forces people to take notice. It could rapidly turn into an exemplary story demonstrating "how we treat customers." Naturally one can create similar exemplary behavioral stories toward staff. If one is deliberately setting out to create stories as exemplars it requires great care. It is not always easy to foresee the effects a story might have.

The effects of stories and anecdotes: Robert Maxwell and Oxford United Football Club

The late Robert Maxwell created around him more anecdotes than the average leader. An outstanding one had great effect. It tells of the time Maxwell bought a soccer club called Oxford United. Apparently his interest in football was not profound and this level of interest was on a par with his knowledge of the sport. He hardly knew that each side had 11 players.

The legend goes that he attended the first game after he had bought the club. Oxford United lost 2–0. Maxwell, who was not noted for his evenness of mind, stormed out of the ground complaining that he seemed to have bought a club of idiots!

The following week he attended another home game, only to see his team lose by an even higher margin, 4–0. This time he was apoplectic. He screamed with anger, "That's enough! If they can't improve next week they're going to be playing with just nine men!"

The effect of this anecdote was that when anybody joined one of his many businesses that person would soon learn that Maxwell did not believe in excess employees. So managers were wise to the need to remove excess labor before Maxwell found out.

Another famous story about Robert Maxwell, demonstrates how concocted stories can easily go wrong. He was famous for deliberately creating stories which were meant to demonstrate his business principles.

The effects of stories and anecdotes: Robert Maxwell and the lounging smoker

On one occasion Maxwell was striding down a corridor in his office building when he saw a man lounging against the wall smoking a cigarette. He immediately called him into his office and asked him how much he earned. When the man replied £1,500 per month, Maxwell took the cash from his pocket and told him he was dismissed for smoking and lounging around. The cash was in lieu of notice and he was to vacate the premises immediately! The story goes that as the man was leaving the premises, he was heard to mutter: "That's very generous, I didn't even work for him. I work for the office cleaning company!"

Although these anecdotes demonstrate the power of this cultural tool, some might argue that it also shows how leaders are ridiculed. Ridicule can be harmful to credibility.

The effects of stories and anecdotes: Marks & Spencer's focus on customers

Marks & Spencer is one of the world's leading retailers. Although its base has been mainly in the UK, it has an international reputation for prowess in maximizing turnover per square foot of sales space and for giving the customer value for money.

One of the stories which plays an important part in the effectiveness of Marks & Spencer's high level of customer care is based upon the day when Lord Sieff, grandson of one of the founders of the business, was standing at the checkout counter in the group's flagship store in London's Oxford Street. He noticed a long line of people building up at the checkout while several staff members were busy nearby discussing how to complete a particular piece of paperwork from head office.

Lord Sieff realized that the head office managers were partly respon-sible for those employees being distracted from their prime function of looking after the customer because they were the people asking for the information the paperwork was intended to supply.

The next morning he began a revolution by insisting that everybody should throw away every piece of paper in head office. From that day onward he wanted a zero based approach to all bureaucracy. Any request from head office for information would have to be shown to be necessary before a request went to a store.

The story had two important effects. It saved millions of pieces of unnecessary paperwork being completed by staff in the stores. Even more importantly, it brought home to sales staff that their first job was to look after the customers who made it possible for the company to make profits. Filling in pieces of paper was only a necessary evil and should never take precedence over customer care.

Additional reading for this chapter

R. Adams, J. Carruthers, and S. Hamil, *Changing Corporate Values*, Kogan Page, London, 1991

T. E. Deal and A. A. Kennedy, *Corporate Cultures*, Addison-Wesley, Reading, Massachusetts, 1982

C. Handy, *Understanding Organisations* (4th edn), Penguin, London, 1993

T. J. Peters and R. H. Waterman, *In Search of Excellence*, Harper & Row, New York, 1982

F. Trompenaars, *Riding the Waves of Culture*, Economist Books, London, 1993

H. Vroom and E. L. Deci, *Management & Motivation*, Penguin, Harmondsworth, Middlesex, 1979

THE CULTURE WORKOUT

Culture is "the way we do things around here." Complete each of the following categories with the most important features under each category. It is important to note the effect of each subject. E.g. for past leaders, put their name – but also what behaviors remain in the organization because of the way they did things when they were the leader.

HISTORY

Event 1 _____

Effect of event 1 _____
_____

Event 2 _____

Effect of event 2 _____
_____

Event 3 _____

Effect of event 3 _____
_____

What is the most important feature of the mental environment?
_____
_____

What is its cultural effect? _____
_____

THE CULTURE WORKOUT (cont.)

LEADERSHIP ISSUES

1 The past leader
Name the most memorable past leader _____

What behavior is still attributable to him/her? _____

_____

2 The current leader
Name the current main leader _____

What particular qualities do you associate with him/her? _____

_____

What is the physical environment of head office? _____

_____

What is the physical environment of the rest of the organization? _____

_____

TECHNOLOGY OF THE ORGANIZATION

Which of the following technologies applies to the organization?
(Check whichever one of the following pairs applies to your organization.)

☐ Paper based	or	☐ Computer based
☐ Batch technology	or	☐ Process technology
☐ National scale of operations	or	☐ International scale
☐ Mature industries	or	☐ New industries
☐ Product	or	☐ Service

What culture effect does each of those you have checked off have upon the organization? _____

_____

_____

THE CULTURE WORKOUT (cont.)

The way people behave in the organization is learned through the stories and anecdotes they hear when they join and while they remain. Try to think of those which have affected the way you behave:

MYTHS *(These are stories which are probably untrue but which get told anyway.)*

What is the best known myth in the organization?

_____

_____

LEGENDS *(These are stories which have sources long buried in the past, but which get passed on anyway, with variations.)*

What is the best known legend in the organization?

_____

_____

STORIES *(These are just the probably true stories you are told to explain how to do things around here.)*

What is the best known story in the organization?

_____

_____

ANECDOTES *(These are entertaining stories which also teach.)*

What is the best known anecdote in the organization?

_____

_____

Value Chains and How to Analyze Them

Definition and examples of value chains

Methodology to analyze all forms of chain

Rationale for and against each form, manufacturing, wholesale, and retail

---

Debate about vertical integration, upwards and downwards

Every product, service, and industry has its own unique pattern. This is formed from the qualities of the product, the businesses that manufacture it, and the customers who buy it. All the ingredients, from finding raw materials to selling to the final user, are known as the value chain.

*Each part of the value chain has its own skills, distribution systems, and profit level. Each part will also have competitors supplying, so that a business can choose to carry out a segment for itself – or buy it from another supplier. This is what is referred to when one considers moving backwards or forwards along the supply chain and is the most common form of strategic growth. This is called the **horizontal value chain**.*

*Almost every product or service has a competitive product which customers compare it to when deciding what to buy. In every segment those products and services extend upwards or downwards. I am suggesting that the concept of the value chain refers to those other products and services which are similar to the business's own portfolio. An organization can also move upwards or downwards along the vertical portfolio to find growth opportunities. This is called the **vertical value chain**.*

Value chain analysis is, fundamentally, a creative and robust way to formulate a growth or market expansion strategy. It may help an organization exploit its traditional or core competencies or suggest ideas for growth which set an agenda to acquire competencies it may need to own or control.

"Do not enter a state that pursues dangerous courses, nor stay in one where the people have rebelled. When the (good) Way prevails under heaven, then show yourself; when it does not prevail, then hide. When the (good) Way prevails in your own land, count it a disgrace to be needy and obscure; when the (good) Way does not prevail in your land, then count it a disgrace to be rich and honored."

From Book viii, tract 13 of the "Analects of Confucius", Arthur Waley's translation, in George Allen and Unwin, London, 1938

Definition of value chains

The creation of any product involves a similar set of actions no matter what the product or service. One has to find raw materials, fashion them into components, assemble the components to make the finished product, distribute the product or service to a final point of sale, and, lastly, somebody has to sell them to the final user.

The names of these five stages of what I call *the value chain* of any business are:

- Stage One – Finding raw materials
- Stage Two – Manufacture of components
- Stage Three – Assembly of final product
- Stage Four – Distribution to retailer
- Stage Five – Retail to final user.

The stages named above describe what can be called *the horizontal value chain*. It is called a value chain because each stage of the process "adds value" to the final product. Each part of the process often has a different set of constituent parts and skills and makes a different level of profits. An examination of the complete line of a product, from creation of a service or product via a search for raw materials right through to the sale to a final user, actually facilitates an extended look at everything to do with one's own business interests in the product. The importance of the concept is that it often also offers any business an easy, relevant means of expanding itself, improving its profitability or discovering where it is vulnerable to strategic attack. If readers work through the following examples, they will soon understand the concept.

For the moment I invite the reader to think about any single stage of the five stages described above. In each stage there is likely to be a range of competitors, each of which supply the same or similar products to the same or similar customers. Take the raw materials stage, for example. It might refer to the farm production of wheat. In that particular business there are many suppliers, each of whom produces almost exactly the same product as that of every other supplier or competitor in that stage. Those other suppliers are the competitors in the vertical value chain. In most cases they will all be other farmers.

Move on to consider Stage Two, the manufacture of components. Continuing with wheat as the Stage One product, the meaning of Stage Two might be the milling of the wheat into flour. Once again, there are many suppliers who will provide this service. Some are likely to be farmers, from Stage One, who have decided to expand by moving into Stage Two milling. A Stage Two miller could grow, vertically, by taking over other millers. If we consider Stage Three, there will be many different businesses which buy flour from Stage Two businesses. To keep it simple, there will be bread, cake, and roll manufacturers. All these will be specializing in Stage Three of the process of manufacture of their product. It is obvious that somebody making cakes can probably make bread with the same equipment. If they did so, that would be a move along the vertical chain. The business may accomplish this by taking over the other businesses in the same stage or competing with them by using its own machines for two purposes or by buying new machines specifically for this purpose.

If we then consider Stage Four, each of the Stage Three businesses may sell their bread, cakes, or rolls to Stage Four specialists in the wholesale or transport industry, or they may choose to own trucks and do their deliveries for themselves, on their own transport. Thus they would cover the Stage Four needs for themselves. However, many will have decided that wholesale distribution is best left to specialists with truck, road, and delivery skills. They will buy this stage from the transportation business specialist.

Finally, there would be Stage Five wholesalers and other specialists, which will break up the large quantities of the cakes, rolls, and loaves from warehouses for delivery into shops for sale to the final consumer. In Stage Five there will be many different competing firms. For example, there will be supermarkets, corner shops, caterers, and sandwich bars in major cities. The businesses in this stage all specialize in knowing the different final retail users who get the product to the "eating" consumer. There, once again, vertical growth could come from a big business which usually only sells loaves and cakes to the public, deciding to also open, in its back room, a sandwich bar, in order to increase its profits and find new customers. Once again, that would be vertical growth within the same stage of the industry.

The different starting points of value chains

The reason to refer to *value chains* and not to *product manufacturing chains* is that the exercise has the objective of covering all types of businesses whatever their stage in the process of business life. The analysis aims to enable the strategic analyst to:

● understand the vulnerability of their own business;
● discover, examine, and evaluate opportunities to grow the business;
● look for increased margins;
● understand more profoundly one's suppliers, customers, and competitors.

Figure 5 shows the layout for a value chain analysis of the entertainment industry. A brief study of this figure demonstrates that the highest margin in the entertainment industry (according to my highly simplified example) is in Stage Two/Component manufacture, in the form of film making. The next best profit levels are found in Stage Five/Retail to final user. However, both stages are subject to the highest risks and most difficult factors. Stage Two is highly dependent upon talent, a notoriously difficult predictive variable. The magic mix of the ingredients of a film such as choosing the director, the actors, and the story seem to be the key variables for great or terrible films. It is highly idiosyncratic. The second stage is dependent upon the previous growth and development of market share. Thus, with regard to the higher margins of Stage Five, whether you are a single cinema owner or the manager of multiplex groups, then you have to read both fashion and your local markets exceptionally sensitively. Making high profits is dependent upon building sufficient market share to ensure that when a great film is available, you are not forced to share the profits with other owners.

	Stage One	Stage Two	Stage Three	Stage Four	Stage Five
	Finding raw materials	*Manufacture of components*	*Assembly of final product*	*Wholesale distribution*	*Retail to final user*
	Film	Outdoor sets	Film processing	Physical distribution to showing venues	Multiplex cinemas
	Lighting	Studios	Film cutting	Packaging for film channels	Single cinemas
	Cameras	Film making	Film copying	Sales to outlets (cinema groups, single cinemas)	Cable TV
	Trolleys		Dubbing	Packaging for aerial TV	Satellite TV
	College training of technicians		Subtitling		Aerial TV
Typical profit level range	10%	0–1000%	7–10%	10–12%	12–20%
Typical risk	Low	High	Low to medium	Medium	Medium
Key factors	Glamorous/hopeful	Cyclical/talent dependent	Technical/connections	Contacts/market share	Fashion dependent /market penetration

Figure 5 A simplified value chain of the entertainment industry

	Stage One	Stage Two	Stage Three	Stage Four	Stage Five
	Finding raw materials	Manufacture of components	Assembly of final product	Wholesale distribution	Retail to final user
	Food suppliers	Office buildings	Managing live warehouses	Total warehouse and distribution companies	Offices
	Non-food suppliers	Intelligent warehouses			
	Trucks	Distribution software	Road logistics management systems	Single unit operators	Internet distributors
	Trailers	Traffic management systems			
	Ships	Pallets	Haulage	Multiple groups	Mail order houses
	Airplanes	Trained personnel			
	Tractor units		International logistics	Shipping specialists	Industrial distributors
	Railways			Rail specialists	
	Warehouse buildings			Air specialists	Retail shops
Typical profit level range	12%	15%	5%	5%	10–20%
Typical risk	Medium	Medium	Low	Low	High
Key factor	Someone else's problem	Little credibility without practical experience of Stage Three	Not a lot of benefit from size	Low barriers to entry	Dependent upon understanding retail customers

Figure 6 A simplified value chain of the physical distribution industry

Figure 6, showing the value chain of the physical distribution industry, demonstrates that the profit margins tend to be closely correlated with the risk involved. They are also closely linked to the barriers to entry, levels of technology, "Stage know how", and level of competition. However, it is obvious that the best margins of profit in this value chain for the distribution industry are in setting up systems for clients (Stage Two) and final marketing to customers (Stage Five). Back in the 1980s, the National Freight Company (later NFC) was a leading distribution (Stage Four) company. It had achieved over £2 billion revenue and £150 million profits before tax, per annum. When its leaders undertook a strategy review, I urged them to gain a deeper understanding of Stage Five, final retail systems and marketing. This was for two reasons. The first was that there were much better margins in it. But I also felt there was a great opportunity to find new customers. As retailers expanded internationally around the world, if a distribution company understood marketing distribution, it could set up and work with new entrants to national markets. As retailers enjoy a higher margin of profits in that Stage Five activity, the efforts of the transport supplier (in this case it would have been the NFC), would mean the Stage Four business could share in the increased profits of the retailer.

Differences between value chain components

Each component in the value chain has different problems. It also affords multiple opportunities. I will examine each component in turn.

Stage One: finding raw materials

The meaning of the term *raw materials* differs between industries. Raw materials in some industries (e.g. steel making) might refer to the actual mining of the necessary metals. In others the same stage might refer to the creation of totally finished goods. For example, one of the Stage One (raw materials) for the distribution industry is the finished truck, ready for the road. If we were looking at the truck manufacturing industry, that would be Stage Three in the value chain analysis. It also demonstrates that this analytical tool is thoroughly subjective. It should contain what you consider relevant. Consider a simple value chain – the floor coverings industry in the UK.

The value chain of the UK floor coverings industry

Figure 7 demonstrates that the two places NOT to be in the floor coverings industry are Stage One (raw materials) and Stage Four (physical distribution). While working with a client (which was firmly entrenched in Stage Four) it became obvious that the only way to increase the value of the business and grow the wealth of the shareholders was to:

1 Create brands which would enable the business to capture 1–3 percent of the retail Stage Five's profitability (the business could not actually move into Stage Five because it had been told by the DTI that it would be considered monopolistic and leaders of the business believed it would offend their retail customers).

2 Integrate backwards into carpet manufacturing (Stage Three in the analysis) to increase the profit rate of the business.

The two strategies above were calculated to increase the revenue of the business by 60 percent in two years from £350 million to £560 million per annum. The profit rate would increase by about 2 percent from 7 percent to 9 percent+. It was estimated that would increase the Stock Exchange value of the company from a capitalization of £150 million to £450 million in those two years, thus trebling the value of the business for its shareholders. It would also increase employment for many in the industry. Finally it would give great opportunities to many employees who (it had been found in our strategy analysis) were ready for much bigger jobs, if only they could be created within a larger business.

Stage Two: manufacture of components

The manufacture of components tends to be rather specialized. It could refer to pumps (as used in cars, machines, the food industry, etc.) in which case all five stages would look at the pump industry. But if one were analyzing the automotive industry, the only reference to pumps would come as a Stage Two mention. Similarly, with the industry of battery manufacture. If that were the industry being studied, we would examine five stages for the injection moulding of plastics and assembly of lead and the various other aspects of Stage One for battery manufacture, the creation of lead grids and cases for the battery in Stage Two, and so

	Stage One	Stage Two	Stage Three	Stage Four	Stage Five
	Finding raw materials	*Manufacture of components*	*Assembly of final product*	*Wholesale distribution*	*Retail to final user*
	Wool manufacture	Reels of materials	Wool carpets	National warehouse distribution	Large retail chains
	Other natural fibers manufacture	Reels of materials	Other natural fiber carpets	Regional warehouse distribution	Single retailers
	Chemical based fiber production	Reels of materials	Man-made fiber carpets	Small wholesalers	Internet distributors
	Woods	Planks	Parquet floors	Single national distribution	Contractors
	Plastics materials	Pallets of materials	Linoleum	Multiple national distribution	
Typical profit level range	10%	20%	20–25%	7–10%	15–30%
Typical risk	Medium	Medium/High	Medium	Medium	Medium
Key factor	Tends to be large scale	Controlled by first arrivals	Fashion conscious and can waste investment	Low barriers to entry	Not marketing oriented

Figure 7 A simplified value chain of the UK floor coverings industry

on. However, if we were examining the industry of (say) truck manufacturing, then the battery would make a brief appearance during Stage Two of the analysis.

Stage Two is often the part of any industry, which is fairly profitable. This is because it usually requires technological knowledge and proprietary information, which take many years to develop. Some parts may also be protected by patent registration of processes. However, this stage rarely offers substantial opportunities to move forwards or backwards to other stages of the value chain.

Stage Two is often the part of any industry, which is fairly profitable.

Why? Because moving from Stage Two to Stage One usually requires excessively vast increases in the business's investment in capital for land, machinery, and knowledge. Moving forward to Stage Three requires the assembly of exponentially more know-how, which is usually counter cultural to the Stage Two form of knowledge.

A business can often grow best from the Stage Two segment by moving upwards and downwards along its own stage, finding other products and services which are akin to its own processes. The business may grow by increasing the revenue or the levels of profitability, or both. To continue the example used above, pumps are used in almost any industry. However, if one mainly manufactured them for food industries, it would take an investment in hygiene within the manufacturing plant and a special study of food industry requirements, to enable a business to move into the production of pumps for food industry customers. This could be done with relative ease and is a far more feasible strategic move than moving (say) into engine manufacture or food machine manufacture.

Stage Three: assembly of components

The assembly of components is more profitable with very complex products like automobiles, buildings, airplanes, and information management systems. The more complex the product (usually) the more profitable this stage will be, as well as less vulnerable to integration competition from businesses supplying to this stage. For example, car manufacturing, in the late twentieth century, is very much a Stage Three dominated industry. Few of the small parts manufacturers could dream of integrating forwards into car manufacture. The only key component manufacturer that could integrate forwards would be one supplying (say) engines, a major component of a vehicle. For this reason, all the major car manufacturers have their own engine making facilities. In 1998, BMW managed to spoil the sale of the Rolls-Royce car manufacturing business to VW because it supplied the engines to Rolls-Royce for the car. It could not prevent the sale of the other half of the business, that of Bentley car manufacture, because it held no contract for the supply of engines there and that part of the business was not vulnerable to BMW's influence. But, merely by stating it would not supply engines after the contract date, it managed to secure the brand name of Rolls-Royce for itself and prevent its major rival, VW, from bagging both Rolls-Royce and Bentley brands.

Stage Four: wholesale distribution

This stage is notoriously unprofitable for several reasons:

1 it has few barriers to entry;
2 it requires, usually, a low level of profound know-how;
3 it is hard to maintain legal barriers to entry (other than hygiene for food and legal for pharmaceuticals);
4 it is easy and common for Stage Three businesses to integrate forwards to control their own distribution networks as soon as they can afford it.

I nearly always advise businesses which are stuck in Stage Four to integrate forwards or backwards. Just don't stay stuck in Stage Four. The means of integrating forwards are not always self-evident. But businesses need to be imaginative and determined. For example, in the food distribution industry, one can integrate forwards increasingly into food packaging, offering controlled special conditions for delivery and even food layout in retail stores. Many Marks and Spencer suppliers are responsible, now, for not only delivering but also placing stock onto clothes-racks and placing them in the stores. This enables Marks and Spencer to concentrate on its core skill of retailing; it also allows an opportunity for slightly increased margins for the distributor businesses, which are otherwise stuck with margins of 5 percent or less.

I nearly always advise businesses which are stuck in Stage Four to integrate forwards or backwards.

Stage Five: retail to final user

This stage is likely to be subject to the most revolutionary change as a consequence of the increasing omnipresence of the global Internet and web. The effect of this will be that almost all current goods and service distribution systems can be sidetracked and abandoned or attacked by newcomers to the retail industry. It merely takes some business or person to notice a sleepy, vulnerable retail business which is not managing the revolution for itself. Once enough retail and end-point customers have e-mail and Internet systems, almost any business can get to them, sell them goods and find a means to physically deliver those goods or services, which bypass twentieth century methods, such as High Street shops, out-of-town sheds, retail parks, and catalogs. The Internet facilitates product demonstration, credit control, and customer address verification. The goods can be stored in any low cost shed. They can be delivered by the lowest cost means according to customer urgency requirements. The retailer then uses the lowest cost guaranteed supplier of distribution. Any modern retailer which is not currently re-examining the Stage Five, retail to final user, aspects of their business, will almost certainly find they will NOT be in business in five or ten years' time.

So far the costs of creating these new retail Stage Five businesses have been enormous. Profitability will only come after vast investment to enable the newcomer to capture substantial shares of the targeted markets against the incumbents. A prominent example, in the late 1990s has been Amazon, the global retail books supplier. It has become the world's largest supplier of books to retail customers by using the Internet to undercut the prices of the incumbent retailers such as Barnes and Noble in the USA and Dillons and Waterstones in the UK. These groups have been forced to compete, toe to toe, on Amazon's own, chosen territory, the global web. It will be interesting to see if the traditional retailer's knowledge of book retailing beats Amazon's lesser level of expertise but greater mastery of the new retail sales systems.

Examination of Figure 8 immediately illustrates that it appears not to have a Stage Three. One could move what I have called Stage Two on to the Stage Three slot if one wishes. Typically, the higher profit possibilities in the value chain are situated at both ends of the horizontal chain at Stages One and Five. Assembly of the chain also illustrates what, in fact,

	Stage One	Stage Two	Stage Three	Stage Four	Stage Five
	Finding raw materials	*Manufacture of components*	*Assembly of final product*	*Wholesale distribution*	*Retail to final user*
	Planes, ships, coaches, trains, cars, bikes, etc.	Airplane schedules		Internet	Holiday organizers
	Hotels	Tourism shops		Retail shops	Holiday group companies
	Takeoff slots	Internet availability		Brochures	Single holiday specialists
	Resorts	Plane/hotel deals		Advertising in newspapers	Customer segment specialists
	Culture infrastructure	Assembly of holiday packages		Advertising on billboards	Holiday resort specialists
	Service minded population	Customers population segmentation		Database selling	Holiday management
	Willing customers	Brochures		Telephone sales	Internet sales
	Insurance	Holiday insurance		Sales at point of holiday sales	Holiday insurance sales
Typical profit level range	15%	8%	N/A	7%	12%
Typical risk	Medium	Medium	N/A	High	High
Key factor	Expensive capital (hotels, planes) forces owners to "best offer" returns. When economy is poor, these drop below profitable levels.	Innovation is the key to finding new markets		Highly oligopolized but undisciplined and subject to first mover discounters winning	Regular bankruptcies offer temporary relief from excess supply caused by low barriers to entry

Figure 8 A simplified value chain of the tourist industry

happens within the industry. Businesses specializing in transport (planes, ships, trains, coaches, cars, etc.) industries move horizontally forwards along the chain to package and sell holidays as an extension of their basic transport competencies. Similarly, many Stage Five holiday specialists have integrated backwards into owning their own means of transport to seek out more profit and achieve greater control over their final product. In many advanced nations the tourism industry periodically makes higher profits. These are subject to regular and extreme breakdowns of profitability. This happens because businesses in the industry break the "natural" rules of oligpolistic behavior. These are that oligopolized businesses should only compete with each other on quality and service and never on price. Tourism businesses tend to particularly disregard the recommended behavior in times of economic slowdown or recession.

Profit margins and value chains

The pros and cons of value chain integration

There can be no fixed rules about which part of the value chain will make the highest profit margins on revenue. All the usual rules of strategic analysis will apply to increase or decrease them. However, for the specific "workout" analysis, consider the following causative variables:

1 The ease or difficulty of entry into that stage.
2 The quantity and quality of proprietary knowledge.
3 The potential for transferring favorable customer attitudes from one part of the business to another.

A pharmaceutical distribution business getting between the pharmaceutical patent owner and the final customer (the patient, the pharmacy, hospital, or a doctor). The more the Stage Four business can cut off Stage Three from Stage Five, the more profit margins it can achieve for itself from the highly profitable Stage Three pharmaceutical company.

4 High technology stages always make more profit than low technology stages. One can usually increase profitability by making Stage One of the business you are involved in, more technical or technological. However, such changes in the level of technology must always be customer

oriented and cost-effective (i.e. they should make the total package into something that is better perceived value for that stage's customers).

5 The higher the share of the total stage market, the greater the profit level (and vice versa).

6 The more important the stage to the total value chain, the more profitable it will be.

Distribution in the USA is powerful because the vast geography of the United States means that large manufacturers specializing in getting maximum returns by large scale manufacture, will probably allow distribution specialists/Stage Four businesses to organize their transportation. Some distributors manage their own Stage Four distribution. For example, Coca-Cola, the US global soft drinks supplier, is able to totally control the soft drinks industry as a consequence of its stranglehold on the distribution stage.

---

7 The lesser the components' importance to the Stage, whilst remaining a vital ingredient, the greater the profit.

In the merchant banking industry, there is always a need for technical, legal advice to ensure any merger they are organizing is watertight. Although the lawyers make only a small contribution (which they always expand exponentially, as a built-in professional habit), they are able to charge very high profit rates for their small, but vital, contribution.

The vertical value links

Each stage offers opportunities to move vertically up or down. If you know how to make cars, you probably could make small vans or trucks. If you can sell groceries, why not cooking utensils, newspapers, and eventually banking? If you know how to make shoes, why not boots? If you have to fly planes for business schedules, why not fill the empty seats with tourists? If you have to deliver goods in a truck from Ohio to Denver, why not sell the return journey of an empty truck at any price to anybody who needs goods transported in that direction? If you are making hairbrushes, why not toothbrushes? If you know how to build swimming pools for private use, why not look for local government authorities which require bigger ones?

Every business should be searching for growth if it is available. Even declining industries have winners and losers. To be a winner, you have to expand at the cost of the losers. There are always likely to remain some core businesses in any declining industry – you should ensure that your business is one of them. Continuously asking questions in your own business such as those suggested above should be a standard discipline. Beware those jaded members of the business who have been around for too long and who always say "we tried that idea five years ago and it didn't work out when tested." There are very few new ideas in managing a business organization. The key to success is applying the right ideas at the right time in the right way.

> *Every business should be searching for growth if it is available. Even declining industries have winners and losers.*

The horizontal value links

I have already discussed the facility with which you can move from one stage to another and the potential profit from doing so. However, there are also clear constraints and dangers awaiting those businesses that move into other stages, whether forwards or backwards, without careful planning. The questions you should ask are:

1 Are my current customers or suppliers going to be offended and withdraw business from me if I go into their business and market?
2 Does the business have the necessary know-how, core competencies and skills to move into a forwards or backwards stage?
3 Does my supplier or customer maintain its attractive profit margins from its own special, non-replicable situation or can I achieve its higher margins when I do what it does?
4 What difference will a move to a new stage, either forwards or backwards, make to the structure, management systems, information technology systems, and culture of the current business?
5 Will my institutional and other investing backers react favorably to my move?
6 Will other businesses in the current stage follow the business in its move to other stages, thus causing excess supply and a general lowering of every business's profitability?

7 Are there different mores and ethics governing the forwards or backwards stage which conform with or contradict the values of businesses in the stage your business currently occupies?

8 Almost all movements in the value chain will require organizational re-design and restructuring. There are no cases where the structure will be less complex. Are the leadership and organizational systems likely to be able to cope?

NB It is nearly always easier and wiser to move upwards or downwards in a value chain, than to move into a new stage, backwards or forwards. The skills are likely to be more relevant and the necessary changes, both technical and managerial, less onerous.

Final warning

The costs of movements up and down the value chain or along it, forwards or backwards, are usually high. A business either needs to borrow the capital to buy competitors, suppliers, or customers, or learn how to do their know how for themselves. Why are the costs nearly always higher in real capital expenditure than one predicts when starting out on the process? It often takes longer, in terms of time, than you guessed in advance, particularly when compared to goods or services you already know well. There are always hidden costs, unforeseen expenditures and technical hitches that take longer to resolve than the allocated time that you imagined was spare within the organization. The most complex and difficult to resolve are usually problems associated with recruiting and training human resources. You should calculate whether your business will cope with the almost inevitable decrease in profitability before the projected increases in revenue and profits start coming. Will your backers stay with you in the crises? Have you prepared them for it adequately?

Additional reading for this chapter

G. Hamel and C. K. Pralahad, *Competing for the Future*, Harvard Business School Press, Boston, 1994

M. E. Porter, *Competitive Advantage*, Free Press, New York, 1985

M. E. Porter, *Competitive Strategy*, Free Press, New York, 1980

P. Q. Quinn, *Intelligent Enterprise*, Free Press, New York, 1992

VALUE CHAIN ANALYSIS WORKOUT

Refer to p.130. Find your business's current position(s) in the value chain(s) of its main products and services.

Fill in the vertical opportunities for products and services currently being supplied by competitors.

Complete the backwards and forwards integration opportunities from the point of view of:

1 Attitude of customers.
2 Availability of business to purchase or copiability of competitors.
3 Profit margins.
4 Your business's competencies and alignment with the desired strategic direction.

	Stage One *Finding raw materials*	Stage Two *Manufacture of components*	Stage Three *Assembly of final product*	Stage Four *Wholesale distribution*	Stage Five *Retail to final user*
Typical profit level range	%	%	%	%	%
Typical risk	Low/Medium/High	Low/Medium/High	Low/Medium/High	Low/Medium/High	Low/Medium/High
Key factor					

Define the Long-Term Strategy First

The choices between growing, slowing, or dying

How to become a cost leader

A choice of focussing on special parts of your organization's interests

How to find some way to be different

How far forward should the forecast be pitched?

Why well-intentioned people still get it wrong

The broadest parameters of the long-term strategy allow you to decide whether:

(1) to make the business grow;

(2) to keep it stable; or

(3) to decrease its size.

At the level of the individual business (which may be a subset of the corporation), there is another set of choices of strategies available to the organization:

(1) cost leadership;

(2) differentiation; or

(3) focus.

*"One doesn't discover new lands without consenting
to lose sight of the shore for a very long time."*

André Gide

There is not a lot of choice

Once you have completed all the analysis described in previous chapters, you have to decide what the long-term strategy of the business ought to be. By now you will have examined and reflected upon the most profitable parts of your business. You should have analyzed where most of your competitors make their profits in the industry, and begun to focus upon where you wish to concentrate. You will also have examined carefully the strengths, neutrals, and weaknesses of your own business and, finally, you will have studied the culture of your organization. (Once you have defined the long-term strategy, you will be able to decide whether you need to change any parts of your culture.)

Now you have to decide what the long-term strategy should be. That is really very simple. The broadest parameters allow you to decide: (1) whether you wish to make the business grow; (2) whether to keep it stable; or (3) whether to decrease its size (possibly leading to liquidation). These are the scale decisions one can take in regard to the overall corporation. Of course, if the corporation is involved in several businesses and possibly several industries, it is possible to decide to increase the size of some, keep others stable, and sell or liquidate others. However, at the large-scale organizational level you have to decide if you wish to grow, stabilize, or diminish in size. You must then decide whether to grow from internal growth or acquisition or a combination of both. You must also take a decision on what parts of the value chain you wish to grow into. From Chapter 7, you'll know that the first choice is between vertical or horizontal integration. You could decide to concentrate on growing your market share from your current portfolio. However, whether you decide to grow vertically or horizontally, you will certainly manage faster growth if you combine acquisition (for the larger part) with growth from internal resources.

Going for growth

In practical terms, there are not many choices about how to increase the size of the business. First, you can grow it by organic growth or by taking market share from your current competitors (you could buy a competing enterprise and grow the business that way). Similarly, you could buy indirect competitors who make products which are not exactly the same as yours but which compete with your products because they can be used as substitutes for them.

You can also grow the business by integrating backward and buying organizations which supply products or components to your business, or you can grow by integrating forward and taking over your current customers.

You can grow your organization by buying firms which contain useful core competencies relevant to your business and which may have some synergy with your company's skills. For example, if you are in mining, you might buy another mining company, because it has a basic core skill of drilling technology which is missing from your own operation.

Another way of growing the business is by becoming a conglomerate and buying any businesses in the marketplace you think are cheap, even if they do not necessarily have any strategic fit with your own, other than enabling you to apply your management skills to a larger business. However, conglomerates have become unfashionable since the 1980s. Most firms now try to "stick to the knitting." This means that, unless you have some inside knowledge or core competence which is useful to the industries or business which you are buying, then it is probably wiser not to extend your business too widely.

Conglomerates relying on management skills to get efficiency from unrelated businesses, are out of favor because they seem to lack strategic logic.

Conglomerates, which are just organizations relying on management skills to get efficiency from unrelated businesses, are out of favor because they seem to lack strategic logic. Some of the largest in the world, such as Hanson, have been broken up into constituent, more closely related, parts. Another, well-known diversified conglomerate in the UK, Tomkins plc, has also announced it is likely to break itself up into constituent, related parts and float off each part with a separate quotation. This follows years of the chairman and chief executive, Greg Hutchings, attempting to persuade the City that his conglomerate is a better bet than any single strategically integrated business. They just do not believe him.

Stability strategy

If you decide merely to try and keep your organization stable and neither grow nor contract, you have a different selection of strategic actions available to you. You could just do nothing and keep things ticking over. Another choice is to focus on profit and try to maximize it. Again, some firms choose, when stabilizing, to segment the business. This ensures that all the submarkets are looked after individually. An added advantage of this strategy is that if a particular market goes wrong it will not contaminate the others.

It is difficult to hold a business in a stable condition. Invariably, there will be some parts of your business which are in growth markets and others in diminishing markets. If you still want to keep the business stable because the problem businesses prevent you from growing, or demand so much cash that you cannot invest in the growth potential, you might choose selective investment. This will mean developing, relatively slowly, those parts with growth potential and counterbalancing that growth against those other businesses which are likely to diminish.

Retrenchment or liquidation strategy

If the organization is in danger because it has been trading at a loss or its market has been diminishing, there is a choice of response methodologies.

The first of these is to conduct a classic turn-around strategy. The tactics of turn-around are to reverse the normal time horizons of the business. That is to say, instead of looking at the long-term strategy and then, afterwards, deciding the short-term tactics, you have to implement immediate short-term tactics to give the firm a chance of having the luxury of a long-term strategy.

In a turn-around situation the rules are very simple. First you have to recognize that you have a profound problem. Nowadays that role often fails to the non-executive directors. It is hard for the executive chairman or the chief executive officer to face up to deep-seated problems. They are probably a root cause of the problem and step one usually requires them to be removed from leadership.

The removal of leaders who have caused the problems is invariably the key starting point for most successful turn-arounds. Unless the leaders, who are necessarily part of the problem, are forced out or resign, then the turn-around is unlikely to begin. As Stuart Slatter puts it, in his classic text, *Corporate Recovery* (Penguin, 1984), "Most, but not all, turn-round situations require new chief executives, since inadequate top management is the single most important factor leading to decline and stagnation" (page 79).

The second, usually vital, step in a turn-around is to centralize, as far as possible, all financial and budgeting controls to enable the financial director of the organization and the chief executive to be totally aware of everything that is going on, even if it is only bad news.

The next stage in the process of turn-around is to decentralize as many business operations as possible. Every manager, down to the lowest possible level, should be asked to state a target budget and keep to it. The budget should be profitable or cost-effective and ensure the return of the firm to profitability in the shortest possible time. The new leaders need to be utterly ruthless and say: "Now we have centralized control it is vital that you, the managers, give us the profits the business needs to survive. Now we have control over the accounts we can measure the survival of the business as it becomes profitable. We must give you a fixed time limit to return your part of the business to profitability. If you make it we will all survive and thrive. If you cannot deliver profitability in your part of the business, you must understand that your section, at least, will be closed down." If more leaders were able to deliver simple messages like this (and ensure the financial controls allow them to do so), many more businesses would succeed in returning to profitability.

A second retrenchment strategy is divestment. That means selling off all parts of the organization which do not have strategic synergy with the core business in order to raise cash to become a healthier organization. One variant of this strategy is to become a "captive company." That usually means saying to one's most important customer, "We will supply solely to you, if you will guarantee us enough orders (even with low profitability) to be able to survive as your "captive supply company." Basically, this means that the organization becomes a single internal supplier. Unfortunately, for them, many of Marks and Spencer's suppliers have had to become "captive companies," with just Marks and Spencer as the key customer. This means that when Marks and Spencer sneezes, they catch pneumonia. Marks and Spencer sneezed in 1998. It will be interesting to see how many of its suppliers survive the contagion.

Finally, of course, a business has the choice of liquidating its assets to try to return some of their capital to the creditors, shareholders, or owners. It is always drastic and painful to face up to the hard reality of liquidation. However, it is sometimes the best thing to do rather than to go on trading into an even sadder and worse situation.

Business level strategies

At the level of the individual business (which may be a subset of the corporation), there is another set of choices of strategies available to the organization.

1 Cost leadership strategies

You can try to achieve overall cost leadership of the industry in which you are involved. Your objective under this strategy is to achieve the lowest possible cost curve compared to your competitors, enabling you to compete on price against any firm in your industry. If you can achieve the lowest cost you can also sell at the lowest price and therefore be more sure of achieving the percentage market share you are aiming for, or matching and seeing off competitors for price in the marketplace or maximizing profits when competition is at a low ebb.

2 Differentiation strategies

Another business-level strategy option is "differentiation." This means trying to create some degree of difference between the products you supply to the market and those with which your products directly compete. The traditional way to achieve this is to ensure that your product's brand is appreciated, respected, and valued by consumers. This can also deliver higher prices, even when there are no basic differences between your products and those of your competitors. On the other hand, you can try to create real differences between your product and those of the competitors.

In the USA, Walmart guarantees lower prices on a large range of branded and non-branded commodity goods. It has established itself in local markets throughout the USA. It creates stores which attract customers from wide-spread sets of communities because it offers such a large range that it becomes worthwhile for the customer to drive many miles to shop there. Above all, it guarantees lower prices on everything it sells. This guarantee creates the psychological security of mind for its customers to know they will certainly save money by shopping there – and they do not need to shop around in other stores in case something is cheaper elsewhere. Walmart made its name by being the cheapest for everything.

John Lewis, a retail trader in the UK, guarantees to sell at lower prices than any local competing retailer. If a customer finds a product being sold more cheaply elsewhere, the store will refund the difference. Its famous motto is: "Never knowingly undersold."

International Harvester, an international supplier of farming equipment, guarantees to supply spare parts within 24 hours, if your equipment breaks down. SAS, the Scandinavian airline, tries to guarantee getting you to your destination "on time." All businesses need something to differentiate them from their competitors. The more individual and the less easy to copy a product is, the more the "unique differentiator" will lock in customers and profits.

However you choose to differentiate your product or service, the differences should be related to marketing information whereby customers have told you they value the differences you are offering. Differentiating on qualities which are irrelevant is a pointless and expensive blunder.

Chloride Batteries

An example of this was a sales campaign run by Chloride Batteries in the 1980s. Chloride was the leading supplier of automobile batteries in the UK, at that time, and had an extensive international business. Chloride Batteries had a reputation for being "technologically superior." This reputation had enabled it to charge a 10 percent premium above the average market price for many years.

A new sales director decided that they were not selling enough batteries. He noticed that many competitors were advertising and fighting on price. He decided to segment his customers by price too. He, therefore, ran a sales campaign to beat the competition with a slogan: "Good, Better, Best." These slogans referred to three types of battery Chloride would offer for every car. The customer could buy a low-priced, competitive battery ("Good"). He could buy a higher-priced one ('Better'). Or he could buy a premium-priced battery ("Best").

There was virtually no difference in either the cost of manufacture or performance of these batteries – just the label. The consequences of this campaign were startling when the follow-up market research was completed a few months later. The campaign had demonstrated to buyers of Chloride batteries that it made ordinary batteries too (customers had really believed that it only made superior ones). Furthermore, as it was the assurance of the brand name they were seeking, they did not see the point of paying higher prices for the brand if they could buy a cheap version with the same warranty. The consequence of this campaign was that Chloride found it difficult afterwards to convince its customers that it made superior products which merited charging a premium price.

Focus strategies

You can decide just to focus your business on a few key products or services which your analysis and research have demonstrated will guarantee a decent level of profitability. When the UK had one, sole British car manufacturer it eventually decided to focus on just one brand, "Rover," and a small range of cars carrying that brand. Trust House Forte, an international hotel group, decided to focus on just a few classes of hotel: premier hotels, executive hotels for the business traveler, and cheap hotels for inexpensive business and family use. The management intended to sell off all its hotels which did not fit one of its key categories. Unfortunately, the management took too long to implement the strategy and the company was snatched up by Granada, a competitor in the entertainment and leisure industry.

Choosing your time horizon

One of the key considerations when deciding on your long-term strategy is to decide how far forward you want to focus your vision for the business. The key variables in this regard are the size of the business and the type of industry in which it competes. Thus, if you are in the oil industry and you are one of the leading four or five firms in the world, you will need to have very long-term plans with regard to exploration, refining, and trends in international demand for different types of fuel and uses for energy sources. An appropriate time horizon for the longest-term strategies may well be 15, 20, or even 30 years.

By contrast, if you are in male or female fashion clothing, the appropriate time horizon for your business may be between one and three years, depending on how large the business is. If you are a medium to large concern in an industry which is continuously changing, such as fashion, then three years may well be the maximum period in which you can organize the acquisition or close-down of buildings, the purchase of materials and machinery, and the training of staff.

It is important to define the time horizon of your strategy because of the subsequent need to divide the constituent parts of the strategy into smaller time frames for your subordinates down the hierarchy. Research has shown that in the best organizations, the longest or most appropriate time horizons are normally those of the leaders. The managers below them should have shorter time horizons. For example, in a medium-size chemical production business a five-year time horizon might be appropriate. This may be influenced by the research, development, and the technological time spans of the industry. However, the leaders of other divisions may be working at two to three-year time horizons. Leaders will need to subdivide the five-year strategy into three-year subparts for the subordinates at the next level down. Their subordinates in turn may well have to further subdivide their strategic objectives down into shorter one-year targets for their respective subordinates.

> **Research has shown that in the best organizations, the longest or most appropriate time horizons are normally those of the leaders.**

Eventually, the large-scale strategic objectives will be reduced to one-week or 24-hour jobs and tasks for the workers on the shop floor. When you complete the workout audit sheet at the end of this chapter you will see this time horizon concept in very simple form. It asks you to define what the appropriate time horizon should be. If it is ten years or more, then fill in that column. If it is five years, then complete that column only. Then break that five-year strategy up into its constituent three-year and two-year parts.

Integration and differentiation

Two researchers at Harvard, Paul Lawrence and Jay Lorsch, researched the time horizons of people with different functions in a number of organizations. (See their book, *Managing Differentiation and Integration*, Harvard University Press, Boston, 1967.) They discovered there is a "functional effect" upon the time horizon of senior and other managers. For example, a senior manager responsible for research tends to think a long time ahead on behalf of the organization. Marketing managers also tend to have long time horizons. In contrast, sales managers tend to be rather short-sighted in their time horizons, usually because they are tasked with sales targets to be achieved in the near term.

My research, published as a Ph.D. thesis (*Managerial Time Horizons and Decision Making and Their Effects on Organisational Performance*, London Business School, 1984), showed that when leaders ask senior managers to think carefully about **the whole organization's strategic time horizon**, the differences between the functional time spans can disappear. In other words, when managers are careful to ask their people to think in **organizational** terms rather than **functional** terms, they are capable of thinking and behaving rationally in the best long-term interests of the whole organization, rather than pursuing their narrow role interests.

Most organizations appoint one person to be the marketing and sales manager or director. Given the time horizon difference between the long-term marketing role and the short-term sales role, he will be faced with a natural conflict in the time horizons of the two contrasting functions. Usually the shorter will take precedence over the longer and the organization will become increasingly short term and neglect the long-term marketing development of the organization.

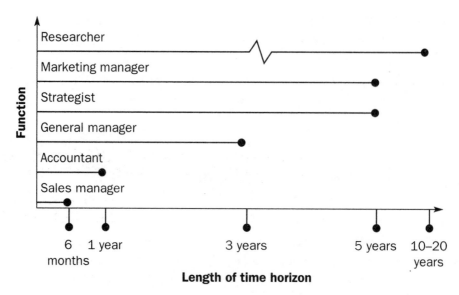

Figure 9 The time horizons of different functional managers

Strategies to avoid

A prime rule in strategy is to avoid "following the leader" in the industry. Normally, the leader will have adopted their particular strategy because it has special competencies. You are unlikely to be able to imitate and beat them. You will thus always offer a second-class service or product if you merely follow what the leader does.

You should also avoid trying to repeat successful formulae that worked in the past. In other words, if the firm's first breakthrough in the marketplace was with a new type of refrigerator, or a new engine for an automobile, it may well be that your next innovation should be a new way of streamlining an automobile. Your real skill is probably in innovation, not new engines. It is difficult to repeat the same success twice, whereas you can use the same competence many times over.

It is also sensible to avoid direct confrontation with your competitors. It is almost always invidious. By and large your competitors will specialize in what they do. For example, if the competitor uses the lowest cost strategy described above, confronting that competitor on his own low-cost territory is only likely to lead to a fiasco and a defeat for your organization.

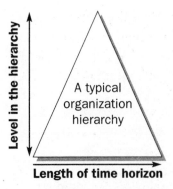

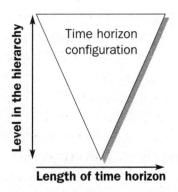

When the time horizons of executives, managers, and staff are aligned, with longest at the top and shortest at the bottom, profitability is enhanced

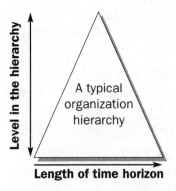

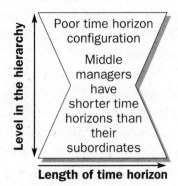

If there is a lack of alignment with staff lower in the hierarchy having longer time horizons, organizational performance suffers

Figure 10 Time horizon alignment affects profits

It is also recommended not to try to do *everything* that *everybody* in your industry does. It is impossible to be the cheapest and the best segmented, and the most differentiated, and to offer the highest quality on every aspect of your product or service. If you try to be everything to all customers, you are likely to be the fastest to disappear completely from the market.

> *If you try to be everything to all customers, you are likely to be the fastest to disappear completely from the market.*

In conclusion, it is also wise to avoid "throwing good money after bad." If you have been investing a lot of capital into a new venture or a new service and after a long and sustained effort it is not working, then stop. Frequently executives think that if they just put another million or two in, it is bound to come right. After all, they say, "We couldn't have wasted £50 million, could we?" Unfortunately, the answer is: "Oh yes, you could and did. It was a waste – and another million or two will not put it right." Classically, the best motto is: "If you are in a hole and digging does not seem to help, stop digging."

Consulting firms also screw up

Recently one of the largest auditing and consulting firms in the world decided it had to improve its billing and control system. It sank £30 million into a new accounting system which was intended to allow the consultants and auditors to keep a computerized record of their chargeable time and also to act (in theory) as an invoicing system. The installation of the IT system had been initiated by one of the most senior leaders in the firm. The system took much longer to design and install than was anticipated and did not begin to meet the specifications and promises made for it.

Consequently, in this highly political organization, nobody in the business was prepared to take on the task of telling the boss that he had led the firm into an appalling and expensive mistake. As the business was run as a partnership, it meant that every single partner had actually. invested and lost £100 000 of his personal income. Every new person that came in to help the firm was asked to do "another special study" to see exactly how much money had to be spent to make the system work properly. It was a standard joke, within the partnership, that "every partner could have had a new Maserati instead of the non-functioning accounting system we are stuck with."

Of course, it was almost impossible to tell the undisguised truth that the whole thing had been a terrible mistake. They really needed to be told: "You have wasted the millions you have put in. Try and find another system and start the whole project from scratch." Unfortunately the chairman's ego would not allow that truth to be uttered – so they continued, fearfully, to try and make a ridiculously inappropriate and poor-quality system work. They might even now be sending out wrongly calculated invoices and continuing to have little idea of what the true state of their business is. It is lucky that, as a partnership, nobody is auditing the auditors!

A note on creativity

Some readers of the first edition of this book have told me, "After I had been through the exercises, you didn't tell me how *to be creative*." My response to that is that you do not have to be terribly creative when dealing with strategy but you do have to be businesslike and rational.

If you assemble the audited picture of the external world and of your competition and then examine your own business's skills, competencies, weaknesses, and culture, and if you assemble the "value chain" map of all the products and services in your competitors' portfolio, most of the creative growth opportunities will be staring you in the face. That is all there is to strategy analysis and formulation. You can see which of your competitors is doing well. Do you want to copy and beat their best efforts or most profitable products? If you do, would it be cheaper to buy the business rather than copy their products? Are any of your suppliers making a much higher rate of profit than your own business? Buy them or replace them with cheaper products of your own. Do your customers make much higher profits than you do in your own business? Could you enter their business and cut them out of the chain? Have you completed a survey (or asked your merchant bank to do so) of all the firms which are direct or indirect competitors? Have you checked whether any of your suppliers or customers are available for purchase?

If you have thoroughly audited your strengths, neutrals, weaknesses, competencies, external opportunities and threats, and your value chain, everything else is likely to be obvious. Now, if you find you do not want to grow in the indicated direction, you will almost certainly have a significant culture problem. Quite often I have found that when companies do not want to take some of the growth paths which seem obvious to an objective outsider, it is because the group has some corporate scar tissue or a fear based in history or mythology.

A floor covering business was in the wholesale part of the value chain of its industry, making around a 7 percent profit margin, while the retailers to whom it supplied were making between a 20 and 30 percent margin. The company was advised to move into retail but feared that their retail customers would resent it. Alongside this myth they also ran at least ten wholesale brand names, all of which sold competitively with each other to the business's customers. When it was pointed out how wasteful this was, they replied that the

customers like having the choices and "they are generally too thick to realise that all the different brands are coming from the same wholesale supplier." It was pointed out that if they were really as thick as the people in the business believed, surely their customers would also not realize that there was a brand new retailer in the market (which would be owned by the wholesale client). Their response to this logic was "you don't understand." In truth they were unwilling to take the risk that their customers were not really thick at all. The practical solution was to build up a good brand for their floor covering products, charge higher prices and grab a little of the retailers' margins by getting the retailers' customers to specify brands that are or will be owned by the client. This would force the retailers to order those specific brands controlled by the wholesaler which would be sold only at higher prices, thus reducing the margins of the retailer and grabbing them for the wholesaler.

Summary

Strategy formulation does not require great creative genius. It requires a diligent assembly for all the important and relevant facts. That is what these workout audits are getting the reader to do. If you do that part thoroughly, the answers will be obvious and glaring. Take those conspicuous routes and lose your fear that you may be missing some subtle, creative route. Most of the great companies have been built by leaders just making the obvious strategic choices, simply and effectively. Others may conclude you are a subtle genius. That is their choice. It is implementation which is hard. That is the reason others have not tried the obvious route – often, they didn't know how!

> **Strategy formulation does not require great creative genius. It requires a diligent assembly for all the important and relevant facts.**

Additional reading for this chapter

G. Hamel and C. K. Pralahad, *Competing for the Future*, Harvard Business School Press, Boston, 1994

E. Jacques, *Measurement of Responsibility*, Tavistock, London, 1956

E. Jacques, *Time Span Handbook*, Heinemann, London, 1964

C. Levicki, *The Leadership Gene*, Financial Times Pitman Publishing, London, 1998

S. Slatter, *Corporate Recovery*, Penguin, Harmondsworth, 1984

LONG-TERM STRATEGY WORKOUT

What competing products and/or services would you like in your own business's portfolio?

_____

_____

Are there any competitors you might like to take over which are available or buyable? Name them.

_____

_____

Are there any suppliers, making superior profit margins to your own business, which you could effectively take over *and* successfully manage? Name them.

_____

_____

Should the firm grow, remain stable, or diminish in size? _____

Which parts of the business should:

Focus?	Differentiate?	Be an industry cost leader?
_____	_____	_____
_____	_____	_____
_____	_____	_____
_____	_____	_____

LONG-TERM STRATEGY WORKOUT (cont.)

What are the organization's main objectives over which time horizons?

Only complete the time horizons relevant to your organization or your part of the organization. Ignore time horizons which are too long for you to contemplate. Name the new areas of interest of the business and state your overall revenue and profit targets for each stage.

10 years _____

_____

_____

_____

5 years _____

_____

_____

_____

4 years _____

_____

_____

_____

3 years _____

_____

_____

_____

2 years _____

_____

_____

_____

9

Organizational Structure

Structure shows people how the organization works

Structure aids implementation

Organizational design is for people to know what to do, for whom, and when

Different forms of organizations described from small business start-up to functional, product, geographical, and matrix forms

The difference between formal and informal structures

*One should only decide which vehicle
(the structure) to use for a journey after
one has decided where the journey
(strategic future aims) is to take the traveler
(the organization).*

"We shape our buildings. Thereafter they shape us."

Winston Churchill

Theory versus what happens in practice

The *structure* or *design of an organization* is the system of reporting lines and job titles that set out the way the organization runs itself.

Academic theories on organizational design recommend that structure should be designed after the leaders have decided the long-term strategy. Theoretically, the advice is sound. One should only decide which vehicle (the structure) to use for a journey after one has decided where the journey (strategic future aims) are intended to take the traveler (the organization). You do not get on a bus and then decide to go to India – you decide to go to India and then probably decide an airplane might be the best mode of transport.

However, in practice, most executives behave differently and tend to sort out structure and design quite early when appointed to a new position. I thought about this discrepancy between theory and practice for many years and concluded that there are clear and valid reasons why real-world practices contrast so strongly with the recommended theory.

First of all, structure and design change in organizations makes for very high levels of political instability, demotivation, and a loss of work impetus. Maslow (see his book *Motivation and Personality*, Harper & Row, 1970) demonstrated that one of the most basic human needs is for structure and stability. It is, therefore, difficult to understand the underlying arguments leading modern theorists (and some executives) to assert that it is advisable to continuously change structure to adapt to the faster changing conditions which prevail in the business world. I contend that frequent change only causes chaos which is never useful when trying to manage an organization or business for long-term profitability.

Similarly, classic strategy theory (see A. D. Chandler, *Strategy and Structure*, MIT Press, 1962), suggested that one should develop a complete strategy for the long term and only then design a structure to enable that strategy to be achieved. Unfortunately, the real world is rarely as straightforward as that. Why do most managers coming into a new post, tend to restructure the department or business first and only afterwards get down to analyzing their strategic purpose or create a plan. Why do so many do it this way, against the theoretical advice? The reasons are mainly related to human nature and common sense.

In the first place, most managers tend to form opinions fast about the people they work with. They rarely change their minds even though there may be evidence showing that their initial opinion was wrong. They thus tend to restructure around their impressions of their people rather than the strategic needs of the business or department. Secondly, most managers prefer to restructure and remove people before they develop emotional attachments or relationships with them. After a few months most managers will have developed relationships with their team members and will find it much harder to look them in the eye when they have to get rid of them. That is why they like to do it early before those emotional attachments are formed.

> The best managers are people who make optimum use of the human resources they find when they arrive, rather than trying to shape the team to fit their own needs.

Many managers make a habit of "taking their favorite sons with them" when they go to new appointments. These are people whom they trust. However, they often need to remove some people from their new department to make space for their own appointments. Great leaders and managers do not need to do this. The best managers are people who make optimum use of the human resources they find when they arrive, rather than trying to shape the team to fit their own needs. Unfortunately, there are far too few *great* leaders around. (see Levicki, *The Leadership Gene* , Financial Times Management, 1998).

The purposes of organizational structure

1 Structure facilitates strategy implementation

The structure of the organization is designed to help achieve the strategy. For example, if the organization has few products but wishes to have a distribution system which covers every part of the country, it may decide to have a geographical structure so that no part of the geography is missed out. Alternatively, if the company has many products, it may design the organization around the different products and the markets it serves. It would, therefore, have managers reporting along product lines rather than geography or function. Very large organizations, where each subdivision may be equivalent to a corporation in its own right, often divide themselves along functional lines. For instance, in automobile manufacture, there would be an information technology director, a director in charge of engine manufacture, another director in charge of body manufacture, and, possibly, another in charge of assembly.

2 Structure allocates tasks and responsibility

The organization design also helps people to understand what their tasks and responsibilities are. If the organization is functionally based, then it tells people which part of the function they work for and, therefore, what their priorities are. In the example above, if you work on the assembly line of an automobile company, you know that your job is to help assemble the vehicle. This also points to one of the problems of this kind of design. If something goes wrong in the engine manufacturing plant, even though with experience you could solve the problem, the design and structure will tend to prevent you from helping. You might, therefore, ignore a problem, even though you could resolve it more effectively than those people who are responsible for it.

3 Structure establishes formal reporting relationships

The design of the organization also designates who shall report to whom and what position people have in the organization's hierarchy. Ultimately, every organization needs its people to accept that they report to another person and are responsible to that person. That relationship designates what they can and cannot do and what they should expect from the person above them, as well as what they must expect from the people below them in the formal structure.

4 Structure groups employees efficiently

There are many theories about what is an efficient number of people to work together. Whatever theory one believes in, one needs to group people into teams to enable them to be effective when working together. Some organizations believe that no more than 250 people can be effective as a working unit. Whenever they grow above this number they find a reason for subdividing the business into another working unit. IBM believes that fairly small units are the most effective in business and keeps to relatively low numbers to ensure efficiency. Whenever an IBM unit grows, IBM splits it to get back to an efficient and effective group number.

5 Organizational structure designates authority, discretion, and control

Every organization needs to authorize each person's level of responsibility in terms of budget, revenue, or power. The organizational structure formalizes that authority and describes who will control people below them and from whom they accept control.

Similarly, structure facilitates the monitoring and evaluation of all the human resources of the organization by allowing management to see clearly what each person and group is meant to do.

6 Structure facilitates communication

The formal structural design indicates who needs to give information to whom. If an organization is structured as a matrix it is easy for different departments to forget to tell others who will need to know what they are doing with customers. In matrix organizations, it is frequently the case that several project teams have different relationships with the same customer. If they do not keep each other informed, it could lead to the undesirable consequence that the customer becomes the proxy manager of the supplier's matrix organization.

Even within the business, the formal structure indicates which department must talk to which, and when they must do so, to make sure that everybody has enough information to do his or her job effectively.

7 Structure maximizes motivation

We have mentioned above that design and structure organizes people into groups which are efficient and effective. The grouping into units serves a further purpose because it is also motivational. The formal structure tells people what the senior, middle, and junior jobs are. It also tells them where the job opportunities exist in the organization. It enables them to see a path for their careers and how they can measure their success.

The 1980s and 1990s have seen a growing trend in reengineering, downsizing, rightsizing, and restructuring. These have reduced enormously the scope for middle and senior managers to move *up* ladders of promotion. However, once this misguided fashion has run its course, normal promotional systems will continue for the majority of people. People also like to know that they are not moving backward in the organizational structure; they will accept different responsibilities, even if the job change represents a sideways movement rather than upward, in order to expand their experience.

Different bases of structural design

1 Simple business start-up structure

Most business start-ups use the energy of the founder and one or two associates to build momentum and some reserves to grow the business further. Consequently, the founding owner and his associates often have to use family and friends to provide finance and labor. This means that they all tend to be both generalists and specialists in the business.

The owner often has to conduct his own marketing research (possibly because he cannot afford to buy it); he tends to do the selling himself (and, therefore, manage the customer relationships too); he often also helps in production and often does the accounts himself (usually when the owner is meant to be having a break from work at the weekend). The essential feature, therefore, of the small business structure is that it is composed of generalists doing many various specialist jobs.

2 Functional structures

Functional structures divide the organization along lines of skills that are needed within the business. They usually include marketing, sales, research and development, production, operations, accounting, finance, treasury, general management, and corporate services.

The advantages of functional structures are that they can foster professional identity and are easy to supervise by skilled functional employees. They also give opportunities for specialization in particular skills and

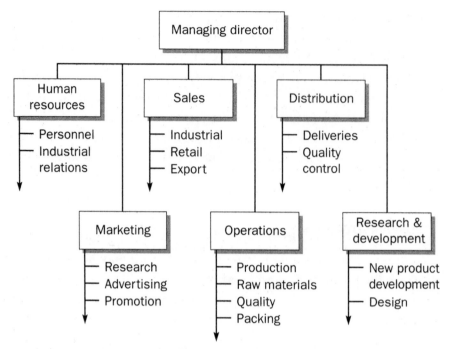

Figure 11 Functional organization structure

provide specialized information and knowledge to other departments of the organization.

Functional structures can cause disharmony between departments. For example, marketing naturally thinks that production standards are not good enough. Production people believe that marketing wants too many varieties and, therefore, makes it hard for production to achieve its own budget target. The allocation of cost and also responsibility for performance becomes difficult to trace. Did engineering fail to deliver a product on time because it is inefficient, or because the salespeople changed the customer's specification?

Finally, and importantly, functional structures tend to inhibit the development of well-rounded senior managers. If the functional structure is relatively rigid, then it will go to the very top of the organization. That means that the senior managers from whom the general management appointments are usually made, will have gained experience of only one functional skill area while rising to the top of the organization. Consequently, one finds that the choices for chairman or chief executive (i.e. general leadership roles requiring an understanding of all the functions of the organization) must be made from a selection of people who only understand a single aspect of the organization. Inevitably, these people can lack balance when exercising overall judgment skills.

One often finds that organizations which are rigidly functional in their promotional and structural systems have to appoint people from outside the organization when they are looking for new chairmen or chief executives. The problem then is that these people have to spend the first few months in their new appointment getting to know the business – rather than running it.

3 Product structures

If an organization has a wide range of products it may be advisable to structure the business around those product lines. This may be particularly appropriate if the products cross different industries and marketplaces.

Most cigarette manufacturers use their cash flows to develop other subsidiary businesses, such as food, insurance, or finance. It is, therefore, appropriate for them to structure their organization to control the different products and marketplaces with different management, criteria, policies, and strategies. The managers in the respective sectors can then focus on their interests, rather than other matters which may detract from the clarity and focus they need for their business.

One advantage of a product structure is that it allows for easy accounting practices facilitating focus on costs, profitability, and possible losses throughout an organization. A further advantage of this structural form is that decision making can be allocated specifically where problems arise. For example, a conglomerate such as Tomkins plc (a UK based international diversified conglomerate) does not really want a divisional person in charge of gun manufacture in the USA making decisions about bread making in the UK.

A disadvantage of product structures is that they can duplicate resources. For example, each product will need a general manager, an accountant, and probably marketing and sales functions. They may also necessitate separate buildings, headquarters, and general staff. This can be an expensive addition to the cost structure of the organization. Product structures can also miss the advantage which functional structures have, whereby specialized occupational skills are developed. People tend to be generalists within their product area and may have less knowledge about particular functions than their counterparts in functional organizations. Another consequence of product structures is that they encourage competitiveness between divisions. This can be counter-productive if the divisions have similar products or sell to the same customers. This problem can be exacerbated in organizations which use the same brand name. Their clients get an impression of wastefulness when they see three salepersons from the same corporate parent. The client will not necessarily appreciate that this is efficient for the supplier (and, therefore, for the customer) because they are selling different products within a rational and optimal structure.

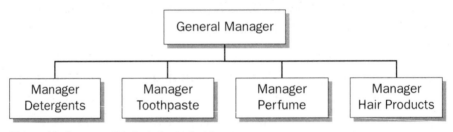

Figure 12 An example of product structure

4 Structure based on geography

If one is manufacturing or supplying bulky or weighty items, where a major cost factor is transportation, it is advisable to structure the business along geographical lines. Similarly, if the market is highly segmented at the local level, whether subnational, national, or continental, it is often appropriate to structure the organization along geographical lines.

Most of the advantages and disadvantages described above for product structures apply equally to geographical structures. An additional problem with geographical structures, especially international ones, is that they tend to build up heavy traveling costs, in the form of both actual costs of travel and wasted executive time. In these structures it is normally necessary to restrict international co-ordination to a few leaders at the top. The subsequent advantage is that these managers become extremely knowledgeable. The disadvantage is almost nobody else does.

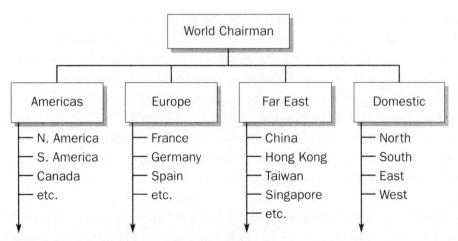

Figure 13 An example of geographical structure

5 Matrix structures

Matrix structures are based on people having separate lines of responsibility. People will have functional and/or product, and/or place responsibilities.

In a logistics business I knew, each functional leader was allocated a geographical country to manage. Thus, the finance director was also chairman of the Spanish subsidiary. The human resource director was the chairman of the Belgian subsidiary, and the managing director in charge of grocery marketing and sales was also the chairman of the German subsidiary.

The advantage of a matrix organization is that it encourages interdepartmental ideas and sharing of knowledge. It also can increase the flexibility in the use of human resources as people sometimes work for a geographical area and another time in a functional role. It tends to maximize the effort that people put into the organization. Overall, it can develop well-rounded managers.

Matrix structures can develop serious disadvantages which make them difficult to manage. There are, however, a few types of industries which use them effectively, such as project-based firms which need to form teams for relatively short-lived projects, or which use several different types of expertise for each project.

Why are matrix structures so difficult to manage? First, they tend to maximize employees' feelings of insecurity because staff members are often not sure which boss they should be reporting to at any given time. Staff can also get caught up in power struggles between different leaders for the use of resources. That forces employees into making difficult judgments about the particular power of their different superiors. For example, a person may report, in a matrix organization, to both a product and a geographical leader. He could please one enormously and displease the other – and damage his career prospects as a result. Matrix structures can also put enormous stress on managers as they try to balance their multiple roles, trying to judge which one is most important and which form of success will aid their careers.

Finally, matrix organizations are infamous for leading to conflict because the lines of authority and responsibility get blurred and lack clarity.

Matrix organization can be recommended in firms which require the constant creation of project teams to resolve particular problems on behalf of clients. Typically, this applies to software writing, information technology, and consulting businesses which develop custom-built solutions for particular client problems. This type of work necessitates the creation of teams which have specific knowledge or skills relating to the customer's business and type of problem. Once the project team has delivered its project and has no further need to exist, it can be discontinued and people returned to their usual roles until called to serve on another project. This

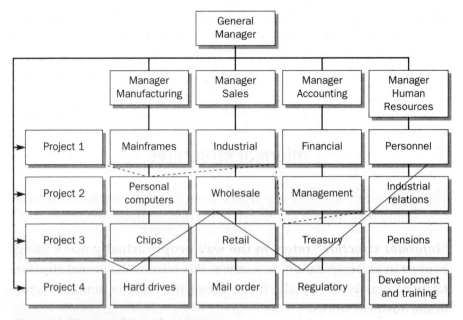

Figure 14 Diagram of a matrix structure

matrix form can be made to work under these circumstances. However, it is only normally successful with a well-educated and highly intelligent workforce which is trained specifically in team skills and where mutual respect is based on expertise, rather than on positional power.

So, what structures work if they all have weaknesses?

Much of this chapter has recounted why each structure does not work. The reader must be feeling bewildered. The problem is that no structure or design is ever perfect. The best structures are those that have been in place over a long period and have evolved to answer business and customer needs. They are usually mixed, with some product and service, some geography, and some functional aspects. They cannot be defended for academic purity, simplicity, or elegance – but they do work. A good example of such a mixed model is L'Oréal which used a mixture of *functional design*, with accounting, marketing, sales, human resources, and production; *geographical structures*, with each country having its own

> **The best structures are those that have been in place over a long period and have evolved to answer business and customer needs.**

HQ and corporate structure; and *matrix structures*, with many country executives also taking part in project teams managed from the global HQ in Paris for particular initiatives in either new product development or special needs, such as improving the IT systems of the business worldwide. An example of a mixed divisional structure is shown on page 162.

Informal structures

The strongest structure in any organization is usually the informal structure, rather than the laid out design of the organization.

"Informal structure" **refers to the way people actually make things happen in an organization. Sometimes this mirrors the formal structure fairly accurately but usually it cuts across the way the formal structure of the business works.**

Most people in organizations like to cooperate and help each other. People do not go to work to do a bad job. If they see where they can help others do things more effectively or efficiently they usually will join in and help, even if the formal structure does not indicate that it is their responsibility or ask them to do it. Friendships get formed as people move around the organization. When their careers move one person ahead of another in the formal structure, they will still retain affection or trust which will encourage them to retain contact and help each other, even when the formal structure could not explain the relationship at all. The informal structure is also the way that information passes around the organization most effectively.

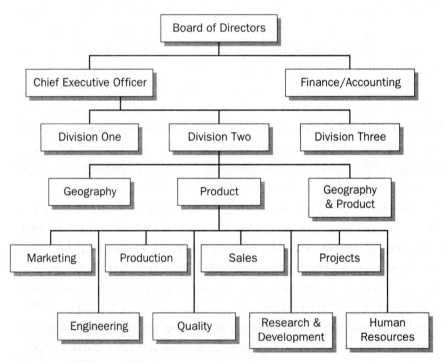

Figure 15 Diagram of a mixed divisional structure

Top Telco – "The Grapevine"

Many years ago I was working on strategy development with the senior managers of a telecom company, a leading international telecommunications business. It was a highly formalized bureaucracy in those days. It had stretched bureaucracy and hierarchy to the extreme, with anything up to 30 different grades of manager. Of course, it could be argued that this was not too many for an enterprise which, in those days, had over 200 000 employees.

However, in order to demonstrate the differences between the formal and informal structure, I always used the following episode with new teams when they first came for strategy instruction.

I would mention two people who had recently been promoted to exactly the same grade and the same title of "director." Both people had received the same monetary reward and each would get a Jaguar automobile to signify his status and importance. However, because the business, in those days, never liked to make people redundant, or to dismiss them for other reasons, it would frequently promote them to a job which could sideline them and get them out of the way of the efficient running of the organization. One could always choose examples of two people where one had received a genuine promotion, or an effective one, and the other had received a promotion which was intended to sideline that individual.

I would test the audience with a question such as, "How many of you wrote a letter of congratulation to A?" (where A was the person who was really being sidelined.) All hands would stay down. I would then ask, "and who wrote a letter of congratulation to B?" Most hands in the room would go up – it was a very polite organization and letters of congratulation were normal behavior in those days. I would then ask: "How did you know that the first person was being sidelined and the second was really being promoted?" Most people would laugh and say: "We just know these things."

That is how the informal structure and grapevine works. People know where power and authority lie, even if the formal design of the organization does not show it. That is why wise managers frequently wait to find out where the informal power structure lies before they start redesigning their organization.

Practical approaches to organizational design

1 Spans of control

Some managers can manage up to ten subordinates, although most are more comfortable with between five and eight. This is a good guide as to how to organize the management and supervisory layers of the business. If one applies these numbers as a guideline to the typical IBM core group of about 240 people, it could be devised thus;

> 240 people divided into groups of eight = 30 groups
> 30 groups could have one of the eight appointed as a supervisor
> The 30 groups could be divided into six sets of five groups each
> Each of the five sets would need a manager in charge
> Finally, the set of managers would need a leader or manager who will be responsible for the overall work of the whole department which is now 252 people strong.

Thus, to get 240 people working, we need 30 of them to dedicate some of their time to supervising rather than working. The supervisors will need managing. The managers will also need managing. Finally, we need a leader to co-ordinate everything. This simple example shows how soon and how easily the potential for things to go wrong happens just because the system needs a structure and management.

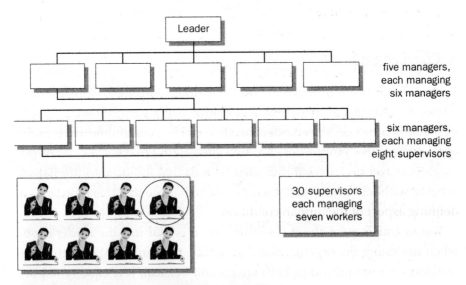

Figure 16 A span of control approach to structure

2 Rationality

Obviously, the spans of control rule is meant to be a guide. If the level of supervision required is low, a manager might manage up to 12 people. Anything over this number becomes highly inflexible. I have met many managers who have larger spans of control. Although they assured me they were managing effectively, one often discovered their subordinates were unhappy and felt neglected.

Rationality also applies to the design of the structure. Some simple rules apply:

1 Keep relevant groups physically together. (E.g. I recently worked with a business where the CEO and the FD (finance director) worked together in one building in Northampton while the chairman, the MD of one (of its three) divisions and his deputy worked in Birmingham (about 60 miles away). I was not in the least surprised when my client's opening statement, when we met, was "we don't seem to have a strategy.")
2 Ensure that groups, or group leaders who are physically dispersed, have reasons to meet regularly to maintain the business relationships that are vital if the business is to run smoothly.
3 If the business is divided geographically, ensure that there are enough people leading geographical divisions who speak to each other and carry corporate strategy along as well as guarantee that the business does not miss opportunities.

3 Communications

If you are an unemployed executive or underemployed consultant, I advise you to start as a "corporate communications consultancy." It will be a surefire success if you offer the clients a free communications audit of a sample of the employees. You will always find that some or all of the employees feel under communicated with or that important information is being withheld from them. I have come to believe that this represents a defining aspect of the human condition.

The serious aspect about communication is that it is the leader's job, when designing the organizational structure, to ensure that the structure facilitates communications, both lateral and vertical. It is equally important to be sure that the culture encourages communications as strongly as the organizational design is meant to facilitate them. For example, I remember working with a global pharmaceutical business which seemed to render its people paranoid as well as force them to work excessive hours. In one ten storey building the company had put easy chairs, coffee tables, and coffee machines on each floor, by the elevator. They were meant to encourage people to relax and talk to each other. However, the seats were always empty because people were so scared about being thought lazy. They didn't dare to be seen relaxing in an easy chair in full view of any manager who might use the elevator.

4 The leader and the leading strategic team

It is essential that the team leading the corporation, especially at time of strategic growth, develops and shares offices together. If a team consists of functional leaders who, necessarily, need offices near the production units or near the sales outlets, there should also be a headquarters building which enables them to spend time together (a day or two each week, perhaps) where they have the opportunity to discuss problems and opportunities and to ameliorate or maintain their relationships.

Conclusion

A great deal of time and effort goes into the design of structure. One chief executive I worked with used to spend almost half a day of every week thinking up different ways he could organize the firm. Ultimately, it was all futile as he did not know how to manage the business.

The final advice, therefore, is to be imaginative and unconstrained in organizational structure design. If it works, leave it alone or tinker at the edges only. Remember that people like stability and even when the organization has to be radically changed, it should be done quickly and then left alone. The evidence is that continuous change is anathema to most staff and executives.

Please Note: The workout form for this chapter is just a set of questions. They will help you to focus on the important aspects you should consider before setting out the structure of your organization on a clean sheet of paper. Think about what you would design if you were designing the structure just to achieve the pure business purposes of the organization.

Think how much you could change from the actual form to the pure form that the organization probably really needs. Then, do just a little of what you think you should!

Additional reading for this chapter

T. Burns and G. M. Stalker, *The Management of Innnovation*, Tavistock, London, 1961

A. P. Chandler, *Strategy & Structure*, MIT Press, Boston, 1962

R. M. Grant, *Contemporary Strategic Analysis*, Blackwell, Oxford, 1995

C. J. Levicki, *The Ledership Gene*, Financial Times Management, London, 1998

D. Pugh (ed.), *Organisation Theory*, Penguin, Harmondsworth, 1971

D. S. Pugh and D. J. Hickson, *Organisational Structure in its Context*, Saxon House/Lexington Books, D. E. Heath Ltd, Farnborough, 1976

O. Williamson, *Markets & Hierarchies*, Free Press, New York, 1975

ORGANIZATIONAL STRUCTURE WORKOUT

What is the size of the organization?
People? _____ Revenue? _____ Profits? _____

What geographical area does it cover?
Local? _____ Regional? _____ Country? _____ International? _____

Does the organization provide many or a few services or products? _____

Which is better known?
The company name? _____ The brand names of the products? _____

Is the organization currently centralized? _____ or decentralized? _____

Are there lots of rules? _____ Or very few rules? _____

What is the proportion of managers to workers? _____

How do you communicate?
Verbally? _____ Written messages? _____ Electronic mail? _____

Does the organization offer the same service all the time? _____

Does almost every order require a different process? _____

How is the organization structured now?
Functional ☐   Geographical ☐   Product ☐   Matrix ☐   Mixed ☐

What is the average span of control (span of control = the number of people managed by each manager), at each level in the hierarchy of the business?

_____

Are there rational reasons for the differences between levels in the hierarchy?

_____

ORGANIZATIONAL STRUCTURE WORKOUT (cont.)

How many direct supports does the leader have? _____

What is the total number of employees? _____

What is the total number of operators, meaning people with direct "doing" jobs?

_____

What is the total number of supervisors and managers? _____

Can you design a structure which decreases the number of managers?

_____

_____

What are the major advantages of your design?

_____

_____

What are the major disadvantages of your design?

_____

_____

Please think about all the answers you have written above. Although they will not give an automatic answer, they will guide you to the way one could ideally structure the organization.

Short-Term Tactics to Build the Long-Term Strategy

The difference between strategy and tactics

Principles of tactics

Good and bad tactics and why

The advice is that the long-term strategy be created first, then the structure should be designed; only then should tactics (the shorter-term priorities) be formulated. Each of the short-term tactics must form one of the key blocks to build the long-term "building."

"How did we ever get to be the largest retailer in the world? ... we figured out a way to grow, and stay profitable, and there was no logical place to stop."

From *Made in America*, the autobiography of
Sam Walton (the founder of Walmart)

The difference between tactics and strategy

Throughout this book we have differentiated between the words *strategy* and *tactics*. Strategy, in the vocabulary of this book, refers to the long-term objectives and mission of the organization. These may cover a period of between two years for relatively small organizations and up to 30 years for very large enterprises involved in extremely large development projects (such as major oil corporations). Tactics is used, as a term, to refer to shorter-term plans of one to two-year periods. These *shorter-term tactics* when added together, over the course of years, will achieve the *long-term strategic objectives*.

The rule for setting short-term tactics

Short-term tactics are intended to achieve the overall long-term strategic objectives when each of the individual tactical priorities is integrated. Each tactical priority should make a contribution toward the total strategy of the organization. The advice is that the long-term strategy be created first, then the structure should be designed, only then should tactics (the shorter-term priorities) be formulated. They should always be subsidiary to the strategy because you should not try to grow the business from tactics into strategy – only the other way round. Many organizations I have come across work almost entirely on the short term, believing that if they get through this year or next year successfully, the long term will evolve out of the short-term tactical gains. I believe this explains why so many organizations go from crisis to crisis, rather than achievement to larger achievement. To repeat, for emphasis, *the short-term tactics must flow from the long-term objectives and never vice versa.*

It is also worth noting that we mean "short-term" and not "short-sighted." Tactics should be part of the growth plan and not based on just achieving this year's budget. All middle and senior managers should know how to achieve short-term results if they need to. It is easy to achieve a budget target by shortsighted behavior. For example, failing to develop and train staff, failing to repair and maintain property as it deteriorates, using lower specification on product manufacture, or reducing the long-term promotion and advertising budgets are all methods used by some managers to deliver budgets without responsibility. Many careers have been built on such shortsighted budgetary achievements. It is essential to develop tactics which achieve the short-term budgetary considerations but do not sell the organization's long-term future down the river.

Fluffy cushion syndrome

I first created this concept when I worked with Chloride Batteries, a UK supplier of batteries to both the automobile and manufacturing industries. I was first called in to help with what they thought was a sales problem. That year the factory had produced 1.5 million batteries, but had only sold 1.4 million. It was carrying 100 000 stock for six months – and it was costing too much.

The following year the business again made 1.5 million batteries. This time we devised a new sales campaign and got orders for 1.5 million. Unfortunately, the distribution system let the team down, failed to deliver 100 000 batteries and annoyed the customers.

The following year the managing director checked production capacity. He realized that the factory could manufacture 1.6 million if they reorganized the runs on the machines and did not change the jigs quite so often. So that year they manufactured 1.6 million. Now we thought we understood the problem. So, we motivated the sales staff to sell the 1.6 million we were making; we ensured that the distribution system could deliver the 1.6 million when needed, in the middle of the winter. Unfortunately, we then discovered the factory had insufficient "refreshing" machinery (older batteries need refreshing before delivery or they arrive flat). Once again, 100,000 customers failed to get the Chloride battery they wanted. The following year the battery refreshing problem was solved. But something went wrong with sales and the sales force only sold 1.5 million of the potential 1.6 million that were being made. So, they were stuck with 100 000 batteries, which looked exactly like the sales problem we started with, three years earlier. We were back to square one.

After three years of this assignment I realized we had a "fluffy cushion syndrome." You know, when you have a real feather, fluffy cushion – every time you try to fluff it to make it look nice, wherever you hit it to smooth it out, it just fluffs out on the other side. You can never get it completely smooth.

Bad tactical decisions in organizations are like that – if they are ill-chosen, they just cause an obverse problem the following year. Good tactical choices make a contribution to the long term and leave no short-term hostages to fortune.

Tactics must be measurable and unambiguous

It is advisable to choose not more than two to four tactical objectives for subordinates to achieve. They should always be measurable in arithmetical or numerical terms. Thus, "beating last year's result" is an inappropriate target. "Beating last year's budget of $25 million profit by 10 percent to deliver exactly $27.5 million in profits by the end of the year, March 31st" is an accurate and measurable target. All short-term tactics should be set in a measurable form like that.

You should also ensure that the tactical priorities are compatible with each other. For example, to ask your sales manager to achieve customer awareness of the product but decrease his budget on promotional expenditure by 10 percent is clearly counter-productive. When you do your review with him at the end of the year, you might find a reduction in customer awareness from 27 percent down to 25 percent. If you wish to use that to withhold his bonus, the manager may legitimately respond by reminding you that he was asked to reduce the advertising and promotional budgets by 10 percent. Indeed, he may have overachieved by

> *You should ensure that tactical priorities are compatible with each other.*

reducing budgets by 12 percent. Can he legitimately claim his bonus? If a manager sets ambiguous or incompatible targets, they should not be surprised if they are eventually obliged to pay bonuses for inadequate performance at the end of the year.

I firmly believe that all objectives can be reduced to measurable numbers. For example, customer satisfaction can be measured by the number of telephoned and written complaints. Production quality might be measured by the number of claims made on warranty or the cost of reworking products which fail factory tests before despatch. Management efficiency can be measured by production numbers, profitability, budget accuracy and staff turnover.

Budgets and tasks

A short-term tactic should, whenever possible, have a budget number attached to it. The budget should be couched in terms of how much revenue must be achieved or what maximum costs are permitted for a given quantity of output or sales. Tactics, being a subpart of the overall strategy, should be determined by the needs of the long-term strategy. If it is possible to benchmark them against competitive standards, particularly competitors who are beating your organization in the market, then so much the better.

Criteria for short-term objectives

1 Increasing or decreasing manufacturing capacity

If the overall strategy of the organization is to move out of one sector and into another, it may be appropriate to decrease manufacturing capacity in one part of the business as it transfers resources to another. Other reasons for increasing or decreasing manufacturing capacity will be to try to achieve product cost leadership in a sector or to become a more sales and less manufacturing oriented organization. An organization may discover that it can buy in its products more economically than manufacturing them in-house. This should lead to a decrease in manufacturing capacity to cut expenditure and release resources for other parts of the budget such as marketing.

2 Improved technology

The improvement of technology is a difficult short-term tactic because technology is complex and cannot easily be improved in the short run. Technology can only be improved at the same rate as the human resources that run the technology can upgrade their skills. That type of training requires development programs which rarely show results in the one-year time spans that are relevant to short-term tactics. However, it could form part of a two-year strategic objective.

3 Increasing or decreasing the workforce

This particular tactic has been prevalent during the 1990s and has dominated the tactical planning of many organizations. Whether re-engineering, downsizing, or rightsizing – decreasing the workforce is rarely the panacea that it is claimed to be by the reengineering consultants who specialize in these techniques.

Given the social and legal constraints that prevail in many advanced industrial nations, the costs of decreasing workforces are high. In recessionary periods, the workforce is reluctant to leave and it becomes difficult to select the members of the workforce who should be removed because they are the less effective workers. One often finds that the best human resources go and the worst stay. In addition, organizations which have undergone reengineering frequently find that they have overdone it and have to buy in fresh human resources – usually people who have neither the skills nor the accumulated know-how of the people who have recently been discarded. In many organizations, the easiest target group for immediate cost savings without commensurate damage is the marketing department. In these circumstances, reengineering becomes a short-term gain which replaces the long-term future – which marketing exists to capture.

> *Whether reengineering, downsizing, or rightsizing – decreasing the workforce is rarely the panacea that it is claimed to be by the reengineering consultants who specialize in these techniques.*

Increasing the workforce is also a difficult short-term tactic. Accumulating new quantities of personnel is easy. Finding the right personnel with the appropriate skills and inducting them into the cultural value system of the organization often takes longer than one or two years.

4 Improving quality

Improving quality, like the workforce considerations above, can only be started as a short-term tactic. Quality should always be improved on a continuous basis. Making quality improvement a tactical objective is a useful tool when standards have fallen so low that the organization is in danger of losing all consumer confidence in the product or services provided. In those circumstances, attention must be unequivocally focussed on improving quality to convince the customers that the company has a right to exist. But it should be done as the start of a process that will never end – not as a one-off, short-term fix.

5 Maximize profits

There are two circumstances when maximizing profits is an appropriate tactic. The first is when long-term strategy is inapplicable because the firm is in a turn-around situation. Under these circumstances all normal rules are put aside. Unless the stricken firm accumulates some short-term cash, it is unlikely to survive for any long run. The rule that long-term strategy precedes short-term tactics should be reversed. The objective is to maximize cashflow or profitability in the short run to ensure the survival of the organization.

The second circumstance when profit maximization is advisable as a short-term tactic is when the organization has had a series of short-term tactical successes over some years. These might be aimed at achieving a targeted share of the market or the lowest manufacturing cost profile or a particular level of development of its human resources. If the organization is close to achieving its long-term strategy and mission, it may be appropriate to concentrate on maximization of profit as a short-term tactic. However, most organizations which had achieved so much would probably find a larger-scale mission and an even longer-term strategy to aim for, rather than to merely try to maximize profits.

Great ideas get destroyed with the wrong owners

A multinational engineering concern had an annual revenue of $1500 million but made a paltry profit of about $20 million. It had been established for over 100 years and had a long track record of supplying quality machines to the farming industry around the world. It even kept design records for every machine as long as it remained in operation, sometimes 80 years after it was supplied.

On behalf of the chairman, I undertook a worldwide tour to understand why it made so little profit and to find a fast-track idea to bring in short-term profits to prevent a takeover bid.

When I returned, I reported that the firm made almost no post-installation sales, either in servicing its installed machines or selling spare parts. This was caused by the obsession of the senior managers with innovation and installation. They were not interested in the nitty gritty of just making profits. I estimated there could be up to $15 billion of installed equipment, all being serviced by competitors or local small businesses. The annual turnover in spare parts could be, at least, $500 million, at net profit levels of 30 percent.

I recommended that a new division be created to manage the servicing and spare parts business because the established managers were uninterested. The chairman felt that he could not invest in new personnel when profits were so low. He gave the new idea to one of the established divisional leaders. He tried to implement the idea for a few months, but it was halfhearted. The idea never "grew legs" and the firm continued to make appallingly low profits. It was taken over in 1998.

6 Improved productivity

Productivity is the measure of the organization's effectiveness in producing its goods or services for its customers. This can be subdivided into human resources, the use of capital resources, speed, and effective distribution. There has been an important increase in the amount of information available in the public arena which enables organizations to benchmark their standards of productivity against their competitors, both in their own industries and associated or nonaligned industries.

Benchmarking data is a useful means of setting standards and clear tactical objectives. Again, it is appropriate to emphasize that benchmark targets should be unambiguous and compatible with the other tactical objectives.

7 Create strategic business units

Strategic business units refer to identifiable businesses which can stand alone as a unit serving a specific segment in a market. For example, a general hair and beauty organization, such as L'Oréal, could break its businesses up into strategic business units concerned with face or hair products. These could be further broken up into the strategic business unit of hair colorings, hair treatment, and shampoos. The advantage of breaking the business into strategic business units is that it is easier to judge each one's success or failure and discard the poor performers.

8 Marketing

Once again, although this is presented as a potential short-term tactical target area, marketing should usually be regarded as a long-term, continuous effort. The essential features of marketing are market research, market information collection, product pricing, market segmentation, product differentiation, and the combination of the above into the promotional aspect of selling, advertising, and PR. Almost all of these are long-term strategies that should be maintained continuously for an organization to be marketing oriented. This does not preclude the possibility of using particular aspects of marketing as short-term tactics. The key ones are *increases in sales*, or *increased use of advertising*, or *promotion*.

9 Financial objectives

Financial objectives are highly suitable as short-term objectives. They are specially relevant when aiming for profit maximization, decreases in costs, or an improvement in productivity (see above).

Other financial objectives that are unambiguous and useful as tactical standards are increases in cash collection speed, decreases in credit availability to customers, decrease in credit days, increase in speed of invoicing, increase in agreements with customers for direct debiting, or increase in agreements from customers for cash flow invoicing rather than invoicing after the total service or product has been delivered – indeed, anything which improves a business's terms of trade.

Other financial objectives may be improvements in standards of budgeting or management accounting. These are most useful in turn-around situations when part of the problem is that the information flows are inadequate.

It is worth noting that this area is often missed in short-term tactics. Accountants are skilled at telling everybody how they will measure their department's performance. They rarely bother to measure themselves. The boss often forgets (and accountants don't remind them) that the accountants should have tough targets, too.

10 Workforce training

People development, in general, should be a continuous long-term strategic policy. Nevertheless, training the workforce may also be used as a tactical objective. When used as a tactic rather than as part of a long-term strategic program, it should involve the following:

- correcting areas where specific people skill weaknesses have been revealed;
- training personnel in new core competencies;
- as a subsidiary factor in the long-term strategic development plan where clear areas for foundation training, such as supervisor or management skills, have been identified as vitally necessary.

A further example would be placing a short-term tactical emphasis on telephone skills in an organization where the overall objective is to increase the sales skills of all customer-facing members of staff.

Summary

The list of short-term tactical objectives can be much longer than the suggestions listed above. It should be as long and varied as you wish it to be. The criteria must always be clear parameters, no contradictions or ambiguities, and absolute measurability. Above all, if the organization wishes to use bonuses or reward systems to motivate the whole or parts of the workforce to deliver short-term targets, then the bonus systems must be carefully and precisely aligned with the achievement of given targets. Failing to tailor a reward or bonus system to fit the target is one of the most effective ways of failing to reach your short-term tactical objectives.

Additional reading for this chapter

K. Blanchard and S. Johnson, *The One Minute Manager*, William Collins, Glasgow, 1990

A. Campbell, M. Devine, and D. Young, *A Sense of Mission*, Hutchinson, London, 1990

T. E. Deal and A. A. Kennedy, *Corporate Cultures*, Addison-Wesley, Reading, Massachusetts, 1982

G. Hamel and C. K. Pralahad, *Competing for the Future*, Harvard Business School Press, Boston, 1994

C. Handy, *Understanding Organisations* (4th edn), Penguin, London, 1993

J. Hunt, *Managing People at Work*, Pan, London, 1981

SHORT-TERM TACTICS WORKOUT

Part One – The Short-Term Targets

Using the highlighted problems from the workout sheet from Chapter 5 (see p.87), as well as the long-term strategic targets, especially the two and three-year strategies, decide the key three or four measurable objectives that must be achieved this year to ensure the organization is on track for the long-term mission.

Priority 1 _____

_____

Measure _____

_____

Priority 2 _____

_____

Measure _____

_____

Priority 3 _____

_____

Measure _____

_____

Priority 4 _____

_____

Measure _____

_____

SHORT-TERM TACTICS WORKOUT (cont)

Part Two – The Accounts

To get your tactics into context

Corporation/business/department's total revenue	$/£m	_____
Operating profits	$/£m	_____
Profits before tax	$/£m	_____
This year's profit as percent of net revenue	%	_____
Cash flow	$/m	_____
Assets	$/m	_____

Budget for your department

(Complete the lines which are relevant to you.)

Total expenditure	$/£	_____
Total costs	$/£	_____
Total sales	$/£	_____
Budgeted profit/loss	$/£	_____

Total number of subordinates in the department at beginning of year _____

Total number of subordinates in the department at end of year _____

Total bonus for department $/£ _____

Targets against which the bonus is set

1 _____ 2 _____

3 _____ 4 _____

Part Three

"Breaking Through The Pain Barrier"

Putting the workout into action

How to use Part Three

Parts One and Two of this book showed you how to prepare and complete your strategic analysis. Part Three is intended to recount the various ways leaders, at every level of the organization, but particularly at the top, make mistakes in their strategic leadership or get it right. There are positive and negative examples. The word "leaders" is used throughout this section to mean all those responsible for carrying out strategic analysis and implementation. Where it is a specific level of leadership, I refer to the usual titles, such as chairman or chief executive officer.

Special invitation

I invite you, in the privacy of this book, to be utterly ruthless with yourself. Do you suffer from hubris? Have you communicated your strategy sufficiently with the people who must implement it? Do you listen to people you *do not* like, especially when all around acknowledge their competence? Do you have people around you who reflect your strengths rather than your weaknesses?

This part of the book could be more valuable to those on their way to the top than to those who are already there. Aspirants have more chance of changing their nature. Too often leaders are so heavily "invested" in their personal habits that it is too late to change. Whichever category you belong to, reflect on the ideas, anecdotes, and observations and decide which ones could apply to you. Then decide to do something about it.

Strategy is Easy –
Implementation is Hard

The ways strategy analysis fails

The differences between analysis and implementation

How strategy implementation goes wrong

The subtle differences between chairmen, chief executive officers, and other executives – and the weaknesses of each role

The importance of loyalty

Stakeholder concepts

I offer a theory of failure here.

"He's never been very successful. When opportunity knocks, he complains about the noise."

Traditional joke: anonymous

An hypothesis of strategy implementation failure

Few organizations do much strategy analysis or implementation. Many pay lip service to the idea but little is done. Why? I offer a theory of failure here. I will offer a hypothesis for success in Chapter 12.

Strategy analysis **fails because:**

- **strategists fail to judge the organizational situation objectively;**
- **they fail to balance the interests of stakeholders properly; and**
- **they have poor objectivity about weaknesses (theirs and the organization's).**

Implementation **fails because:**

- **managers do not know when to stop analysis and start implementation;**
- **they do not understand how to be strategic leaders (rather than company managers); and**
- **most organizations and managers are too firmly locked into short-term behavior.**

The beginnings of strategic failure

In theory, when an organization has an elegant strategy, implementation should follow and success be assured. It is rarely that simple. Problems arise from three main causes:

1 People select the wrong strategy.
2 They implement the chosen strategy poorly.
3 The leaders ignore the strategy to concentrate on tactics.

All three problems can usually be attributed to the organization's leadership. First, only the leader can choose the wrong strategy. Secondly, strategy implementation begins with communication. Leaders, in general, can only implement through the communication of their values, vision, and behavior, aligned with an appropriate organizational structure. It is the task of leadership to make it happen. The leaders have to set stretching, but achievable budgets; they have to ensure that everybody accepts the standards of quality for customers that will capture market share and ensure the best use of corporate resources; they must, above all, inspire everybody with a belief in the "achievability" of the strategy. Yet, frequently, the third cause of failure set out above takes over. They get involved in detail. They get sidetracked. They concentrate on the tactics and fail to keep their vision focused on the long-term strategy. Sometimes they just lack courage – particularly when they have to tackle the people problems.

Stakeholder concepts

Stakeholders **are the various groups of people who have an interest or stake in the enterprise. They range from bankers and other financial institutions, to shareholders, debenture holders, stockholders, trade unions, employees, customers, and suppliers. In short, everybody or every group which must be taken into account when deciding what to achieve, when, and how much.**

The key aspect of stakeholder theory is that the different stakeholders' requirements often conflict with each other and those of the organization. For example, the employees want the highest possible levels of remuneration, whereas the shareholders might want lower levels of wages to ensure higher profits and dividends. The organization's financial backers may prefer a low-risk approach to achieving the organization's objectives, whereas senior managers, who may be on high levels of bonus for short-term achievement, might want to take greater risks to achieve the objectives earlier. Should the corporation pay higher dividends to underpin the share price, or higher wages to attract the best employees? If managers believe that raw materials supply is a key to the future of their industry, they might manage negotiations with suppliers in a

> **Stakeholder theory demonstrates that managers and leaders are always making tradeoffs between conflicting demands on resources.**

conciliatory manner. However, if they pay more to suppliers, should they keep wages low or prices high or dividends low?

Stakeholder theory demonstrates that managers and leaders are always making tradeoffs between conflicting demands on resources. This requires fine judgment which, ultimately, is what they are paid for.

What goes wrong?

1 Leadership and management are intrinsically different

Why do so many executives get it wrong when they land strategy-leading positions in organizations? The two prime reasons are related to the type of person who is driven to reach senior posts in organizations and also because the process of reaching the leading job can affect people in harmful ways and render them unfit for the role by the time they get it. Many people appointed to leadership positions were only ever fit to be managers, not leaders. Those responsible for their promotion did not distinguish between the two (see my book on leadership, *The Leadership Gene*, Financial Times Pitman Publishing, London, 1998).

Many more leaders fail than succeed if one measures success by whether they make a difference to the organization. It may be the nature of leadership in the modern era that causes failure. Teamwork is the key concept of management nowadays. Yet the word "leadership" implies the opposite of teamwork or of management. People have to be effective managers to reach the top of the organization. But as they move up the hierarchy of the organization, more leadership skills and less management are needed.

Management is not the same as *leadership*. **It requires different qualities. Managers organize people to deliver organizational objectives. Leaders have to decide what the objectives should be. Managers (apart from making inputs themselves) receive strategic direction from others who are making the really difficult judgments about the balance between the different stakeholders' requirements.**

While managers make some judgment calls, it is those leaders who have to make major, strategic decisions. It is only at the top of the organization, when one is finally in charge of the total strategy for the whole organization, that the ultimate judgments must be made *on behalf of all the stakeholders*.

2 Different ways of failing

A classic example of failure often occurs in engineering companies. In businesses such as these engineers take charge of increasingly large engineering projects as their careers develop. At the higher echelons there will be much more management and less engineering input to a manager's business decisions. However, at the very top of the company, although the leader needs an understanding of engineering they don't need to employ actual engineering skills. That is something to be delegated to others. The leadership role requires the leader to give strategic direction and to exercise wisdom in selecting appropriate team members to devise and implement the strategy. Yet, often, up to this point in their career, the leader has been promoted on the basis of his engineering judgments.

Another route to the top is through the selling function. Again, the leader will have proved his worth by excelling in the sales function, but the final promotion to the general leadership role is often the one that proves to be the "promotion too many." Why? The selling function tends to have the shortest time horizon of any function in an organization. Salespeople tend to concentrate their efforts toward bonus periods of between three months and one year. Consequently, the management of the selling function does not help a person to develop a full range of strategic leadership skills or equip them for general management and strategic leadership.

The common theme in the two examples above is that people often rise to the top of the firm by displaying excellence in just one function, whether it be engineering, sales, accounting, or personnel. None of these, on its own, can possibly develop the capacity to handle the wide range of stakeholders that leaders have to cope with. Furthermore, these skills can *never* be fully tested or proven in advance of getting the top job. This explains why the "Peter Principle" (that everybody, eventually, gets promoted to a job above his or her level of competence) applies most forcibly to those who reach the top jobs.

Everybody has difficulty coping with promotion. New jobs are difficult and each one has its own learning curve. It is only in the top leadership position that the learning curve affects the whole organization. It is also the only learning curve which demands comprehensive judgment about all the stakeholders' interests. That is why it is hard to predict success and even harder to be successful.

3 Leaders begin to believe their own mythology

There is an inevitable process which befalls successful people. It begins at the start of their rise up the ladder. They are often singled out for success. Sometimes this happens because they are mentored by a senior person in their organization. Others are somehow "destined" to reach the top. Some enter fresh out of university and remain "Crown Princes" throughout their careers. By the time any of these people get near the senior echelons of the organization, they have developed a belief that they are more successful than others by right. This is a natural process and applies to good as well as poor leaders.

Good leaders will have reflected on what it is they do, subconsciously or consciously, to ensure that people are led to success by them. Poor leaders may not have gone through this thought process, and will still be managing in a style which reflects innate beliefs about what motivates people to work in a particular way. (If they do not do it purposely, they will have done it accidentally.)

All behavior implies some underlying view of the nature of human beings and what one has to do to get them to behave in a particular way. Successful managers start to think consciously, at an early stage in their careers, about what their underlying principles of management and leadership are. This will lead them to develop a view about what motivates people and makes them want to work and be successful. By the time the manager gets to the top and becomes a leader, he should have a firm set of principles upon which to base his behavior.

> By the time the manager gets to the top and becomes a leader, he should have a firm set of principles upon which to base his behavior.

If he has not thought it through, then he will probably have half-baked or wrong notions of what it is about his behavior that makes him successful. The general flattery that most bosses receive may have convinced him that he really is different from other people. Worse still, he may have begun to believe his own mythology about his role in the success and motivation of his people.

Martyn Taylor had a brilliant career as a journalist, culminating at a young age with him being a highly insightful commentator running the Lex column for the *Financial Times*. However, some business people thought that the capacity to comment and analyze was the same as the capacity to lead. (It often happens to academics, too.) Martyn Taylor was appointed CEO of Barclays Bank plc, the major UK institution. He continued to make commentaries everywhere, becoming the toast of the after dinner speech circuit, as well as running Barclays as his day job. After just a few years of his leadership, the bank had become a takeover target, with poor quality results. Martyn Taylor petulantly resigned when the board would not accept, without strategically analyzed proofs, his latest scheme to get Barclays Bank out of the terrible position it now found itself in. Martyn Taylor remains a brilliant "youngish" man, but now his future is mainly behind him.

4 Is the team more important than the individual?

The eternal question about organizations will always be whether it is teams or individuals which make the greatest contribution to success. The very concept of "organization" implies teamwork. The industrial revolution was founded upon the concept of bringing people together to work in one place so they could be managed more efficiently in their employment of time. Eventually, as people came together to work, larger machines and processes were developed to get greater economies of scale. But the more people worked in teams, the greater was the parallel need for managers and leaders to guide them and ensure that economies were actually achieved.

Management practice since the industrial revolution has tended to demonstrate to managers and leaders that the role of the individual is supreme. Most organization charts are still drawn hierarchically with the bosses at the top and the various workers below (when they get on the chart at all).

The classical hierarchical organization tends to confirm to the rising manager that he makes the difference as an individual. That is why he is being rewarded by promotion and increases in salary.

So often it is individuals rather than teams which are selected for praise, bonuses, prizes, and promotion. The leaders they emulate are also usually seen as all-powerful individuals. In many organizations one hears legendary stories about the bully or the drunk or the half-mad, risk taker who nearly lost the company its reputation but somehow managed to get out of trouble. One rarely hears stories about the quiet person who knew how to inspire others and get people to work together as a team. Even more rare are anecdotes about introverts who inspire people to forget their egos, combine together and who always give the credit to others.

The most distasteful stories in organizations are about leaders who cheat on the system, managers who claim the credit when it belongs to the team or a subordinate, the person who always knows how to claim credit for accomplishments that belong to others. Frequently these people have a reputation for being "good at politics." By the time they have reached the top of the firm, such managers will be confirmed egotists and egocentrics. They will believe that they can fool all the people all the time. Above all they will not have learned the key lesson that management and leadership require teamwork and cooperation.

The great organizations of the twenty-first century will be complex, multinational, and vast. They will probably be too complex for most individuals to understand or lead. The few leaders with the skills to lead such organizations will achieve premium wages and be in high demand. Those leaders will understand that the only way they can lead their enormous organizations is through the use of teams. Those teams will achieve greater creativity, more productivity, and highest quality for more customers. That will be the key to organizational life in the twenty-first century – the combination of rare and gifted leaders with high quality, well-trained teams to implement the vision and strategic mission of the organization.

5 Most managers learn too few leadership skills

Most people learn a few tools of the management trade and then apply them to all the jobs they get throughout their career. There may be a theoretical explanation to this. Herbert Simon, Nobel Laureate in Economics, in his book, *Models of Man* (Wiley, New York, 1957), believed that most human beings are only capable of manipulating a strictly limited number of units of data within their short-term memory when taking decisions. Usually, asserts Simon, this is limited to between six and eight digits of data. Only the very brightest of minds handle more. Empirical observation seems to corroborate Simon's assertion. The kinds of limited criteria managers use are:

"Most people need both carrot and stick to be motivated to perform."

"Manual workers are intrinsically lazy and are only motivated by money."

"Teamwork is the only tool that achieves results."

"Never get angry with anybody and you'll leave no hostage to fortune."

"It is only individuals who make a difference – the herd is there to follow."

"Always get your retaliation in first."

"Pay low and increase the profits."

"Pay more and never incur industrial strife."

"Network like mad, and blow the business. It will look after itself."

"Never repair the roof – put the money into profits. Let your successor pay for your success."

My somewhat cynical (but objective and accurate) list can go on endlessly. The point is that most managers work with just one or two concepts and do not realize that some management situations, at some point in the life of the business or their careers, will just not respond to their limited views about motivation or success. As a general rule, the higher the level in the firm, the larger the range of skills, techniques, and styles the manager will need for different situations.

6 The leader must know his own weaknesses

By definition, everyone makes mistakes; only teams can avoid them.

> By definition, everyone makes mistakes; only teams can avoid them.

Most management systems encourage people to avoid responsibility for mistakes or to avoid taking risks. By the time a manager becomes a leader he may have become totally risk averse. At the top of the organization one has much more to lose than when climbing the ladder.

A further consequence of hierarchical organization systems and the avoidance of mistakes is that when leaders arrive at the top they tend to think they need no further training or personal development. They would never fail to make sure that their company automobiles get a regular maintenance check. But they willingly and foolishly neglect themselves by failing to go for further training at the point in their careers when the company needs them to learn and to know more than ever. A lack of humility in leaders is a flaw which can eventually prove fatal.

I observed this in a major international transport corporation which had been highly successful and was regarded as likely to become a world beater. The chairman, chief executive, and human resources director struggled to persuade the executive operations directors that they needed to close the gaps in their knowledge base, especially on accounting, quality, and IT matters. The executives always avoided the further training they were offered on the basis that they were too busy to divert their attention from the business just to attend development programs. Eventually that $3 billion corporation lost its way, under the leadership of those executives. They all lost their jobs and were replaced by younger, more highly trained managers. However, the organization also lost out. All their experience, knowledge of the industry, and their contacts with customers were lost too. When they joined new organizations, of course, they all had to undergo the training they had avoided so studiously earlier.

7 Failure to grow into the job

Some managers arrive at the top of their organizations with an unrealistic view of their own limitations and a tendency to see mistakes as something which other people commit but which they must correct. Too often the leader arrives at the top with an inadequate understanding of his own weaknesses. When he starts to assemble a team, or make adjustments to the team he inherits, he will often fail to ensure that it covers his worst weaknesses. He may even select people who resemble him in behavior, thus exacerbating any dangerous aspects of the strengths he may have and failing to cover his weaknesses.

8 Fear of excellence

There a number of behaviors which indicate leaders' discomfort when they are encountering difficulties adjusting to their job. Although the behaviors come in many guises, the main ones to look for are:

1 failure to use the best people for fear of looking bad themselves;
2 a massive increase in political behavior;

3 rapid turnover of senior executives, particularly those close to the leader;
4 excessive use of external consultants;
5 creation of new corporate headquarters, usually away from the more competent members of the organization;
6 continuously asking for more data whenever their subordinates push them to make decisions;
7 they suddenly stop consulting their best friends about their problems because they are afraid to confront possible evidence of failure.

A simple case of 'analysis paralysis'

I was asked to meet the managing director of a large food company. It took several months to arrange the lunch as he canceled several meetings at short notice.

When we finally got together he arrived about 45 minutes late. He pointed out that he knew every theory that I knew (he had a reputable MBA) and that his judgment had to be at least as good as mine because he was being paid a lot of money to do the job. Unless I could come up with something original instantly he could not see what use I could be.

I had to agree with his infallible logic. Without being allowed time to learn about the company, I could make no observations, original or otherwise. But, with impeccable logic from his point of view, without a valid contribution why should he commit any time to me? We agreed to go no further.

He had employed the same impeccable logic with all his employees (of whom there were at least 3000). Later, I learned that he had not made a decision for over three years. During that time his office and the corridors around his office had become mired in paper from the computer room. He had been building ever larger databases to prepare himself to take a decision. He never took it.

Ultimately, his subordinates went to the chief executive to ask him to relieve them of their appalling situation. For three years they had been trying to get agreement on various courses of action they had proposed; the MD always asked for more information and avoided making a decision.

His departure became their solution. Within a few months the results of that division leaped forward and it became the best performing division in the corporation.

The special problems of different
levels of leadership

1 Problems at the level of chairman

Many people who achieve the level of chairman in any large or important organization have a nagging fear of failure. Holding supreme responsibility brings to some people the harsh realization that "the buck really stops here." Being in charge is, by definition, a lonely job. Why do so many leaders feel insecure?

The role of chairman is always overlaid with political and organizational connotations. Most things a chairman says or does are imbued with a special meaning by those around him. Anything or everything may be taken by some subordinates as a signal that somebody is in or out of favor. Whatever he does differently from previous habits may be adopted as "the *new way* we do things around here." Anything can give a wrong impression or lead the firm in the wrong direction.

Occasionally the problem may be linked to overdeveloped ego problems. Sometimes one finds the chairman's ego in direct conflict with the equally well-developed ego of the chief executive or managing director, who is probably aspiring to their job.

Chairmen, by definition, should be concerned with long-term achievements. However, if they become excessively conscious of the need to "leave a mark for posterity," they may start to behave with more anxiety about what people will say about them after their departure, than what people are saying about them now. What the firm really needs is to have them develop an appropriate time horizon for the needs of the firm in its particular industry.

A difficult aspect of chairing any organization is judging the balance between short, medium, and long-term investment requirements. Most jobs the chairman will have had before his appointment as leader, will have required shorter time horizons than the top position in the organization. There is always a temptation, in the senior job, to chalk up "a quick win." This is human but unfortunate. It also gets in the way of thinking about the longer-term needs of the strategy.

> **A difficult aspect of chairing any organization is judging the balance between short, medium, and long-term investment requirements.**

Other short-term considerations get in the way of longer time horizons. This happens particularly when the chairman is reaching the end of his period in office and getting ready for retirement. There is a strong temptation to maximize the profitability of the organization. This may be due to a desire to "go out on a high note", or because the chairman's pension benefits are linked to their performance as leader in the last year or two in office. Most chairmen know how to maximize the short-run profitability of the organization. It is unfortunate when they give in to the temptation to go for short-run profits at the expense of more important long-term investments. Usually it is the responsibility of the remuneration or compensation committee to ensure that the bonus and pension system are organized to help the retiring chairman resist the temptation to maximize short-term earnings at the expense of the organization's longer-term needs.

Some leaders just never grow into the role of chairman. Symptoms of this failure may be that they concentrate on too many short-term objectives, or too much on the long-term interests of the organization. (Sometimes the latter is accompanied by the assertion that: "The Board just does not think far enough ahead to understand where I want to take the organization.") The problem is that they have missed the balance of judgment between long, medium, and short-term considerations that must be achieved if the organization is to be successful and thrive.

Nobody can predict with total certainty that a person will succeed when promoted to the next level in his firm. The least predictable promotion of all is that into the role of chairman because that job calls for skills that were never needed at all levels below. The key need to comprehensively balance *all* the stakeholders' interests inside and outside the organization is a level of judgment that will never have been tested before. The job also carries a need for political (with a small "p") skills which may not have been needed before. This is why promotion to the level of *successful* chairman is the hardest to predict.

Most managers dream that at some time in their careers they will be promoted to a job where they start with a completely clean slate. They dream they will have, at last, a clear set of objectives and be able to select a totally new team. This choice, they believe, will assure a total success. The dream can never happen. There are always some people in the team one would never choose to work with. There are always some objectives one would not choose for oneself. Yet, managers still dream of the perfect promotion to an ideal job or situation.

Why do leaders retain somebody who seems to lack the skills for the job?

Sometimes one observes a chairman retaining a chief executive or managing director who appears to lack most of the skills for the job. Why do leaders retain somebody who seems to lack the skills for the job? There are usually good reasons why these relationships are sustained. In the first place, the person may have the skills for the job but the observer cannot see the problems and is, therefore, making a poor judgment on insufficient criteria. Sometimes the subordinate is somebody with a strong grip on the post (and the chairman does not need a fight at that time). There may be a long-term relationship between the chairman and the chief executive. They probably moved up the ranks of the organization together. There may have been times when the roles were reversed with the CEO in charge of the present chairman. They may owe each other favors which observers will not be aware of. They may have a strong emotional commitment to each other which they consider more important than the performance failures. These emotional ties are strong and difficult to break.

When an organization has a poor reputation as an employer or profit earner prior to the chairman's appointment, there may be a genuine problem recruiting good senior managers. Most sensible high-quality managers will not want to risk their reputations by coming to an organization that is performing poorly. This may be the time when past favors and relationships become useful. If the chairman has impressed people during his career, this will be the time to persuade them to come and join a "successful turn-around." He will certainly need people from outside the firm as well as within. They will have to believe in him and his ability to make successful changes – and he will have to call in "debts" from "those who owe him favors." If a chairman is unable to attract the right people to help him turn around a poorly performing organization, he may find himself involved in the vicious downward spiral that sometimes befalls organizations which lose their way. An organization's poor reputation becomes a self-fulfilling prophecy.

Some managers believe that the higher they move in the organization the more decisions they have to take. In fact the reverse is probably true. When senior leaders make decisions, they can affect the whole organization. The higher up the hierarchy one climbs, the more widespread the ramifications of any decision. For example, if a policy decision is made, it may necessitate the rewriting of manuals, the creation of new training programs, and some restructuring of the organization. Many decisions from leaders cause massive disruption in the normal workings of the firm. A useful rule is: "A few excellent decisions are preferable to many small, less optimal, ones."

A sanguine man

One of the best leaders I knew was in charge of a well-known enterprise with an annual revenue of about £400 million. When he took over the leadership, he set out his principles which were basically that he hated surprises and always wanted his people to deliver on their promises when they agreed annual budget targets with him. He promised to back them with resources and never drive them too hard into making promises he thought they could not keep.

In five years of leadership he made only two major decisions (although, obviously, he took many minor ones, like when to hold the Christmas party, what prizes to give to the best workers or manager, and where to set targets for reasonable success in each year's budget round). The only two big decisions he took were, firstly, to reduce the number of divisions in his business from seven to five. This enabled him to reduce administrative overheads, remove two managers who were performing badly, and send a mild warning signal to the other divisional leaders to try harder. The only other major decision he made during his period as chairman was to make no further decisions! He retired with maximum bonuses. He became a multimillionaire. And he was one of the most popular leaders the organization ever had. He also retired in excellent health. Fifteen years later he is still welcomed as a popular visitor at head office or any of the businesses around the world.

Gerry Robinson, the chief executive of Granada plc, a UK leisure and hotels group, has stated that he only makes about six decisions a year, tries to go home at 5.30pm and avoids working weekends. If only more executives lived by those guidelines.

Another way leaders fail is by forgetting to set the parameters of the different roles at the top of the organization. For example, the chief executive and the chairman often assume each knows what the other is meant to do. They, therefore, never make clear to each other, or to their subordinates, the different roles or tasks which they think each is responsible for. This can create confusion for them and those around them, especially if they issue contradictory instructions and policies. The problem can continue for a long time because most subordinates will be reluctant to act as go-betweens for their leaders. This tends to be one of those situations when it is relatively easy to be the "messenger who gets shot."

2 Problems with the chief executive officer or managing director

The titles "chief executive officer" and "managing director" are being used here to refer to the person at the second level in the hierarchy of a medium to large corporation. This person usually reports to the chairman and has responsibility for delivering the medium-term strategy and the annual budget or plan. It is the dysfunctions which arise from the positional problems which are being discussed here. Some of the weaknesses typical of the chairman may also apply to the CEO. This section concentrates on problems specific to the CEO's role.

For most CEOs, the job may represent *the last role but one* that they aspire to – they often covet the position of chairman. Many of the people who get to this level are psychologically, excessively driven human beings and never know when they have reached the limits of their competence. Most believe somebody will tell them when they are ineffective. Otherwise, they assume they will just get no further promotions. Unfortunately, if the desire to be chairman is too strong it can distract from their performance as CEO. They try to take over roles or jobs that belong to the chairman.

The opposite of this problem is not being able to let go of their last job. Some CEOs get involved in too much detail and continue to do the job they held before the CEO appointment. This is not only frustrating for their subordinates, but renders them ineffective too.

Modern management theory advocates flat hierarchies and ever increasing spans of control. Teamwork is meant to magically decrease costs and improve productivity. Of course, managers need to know how to run a team as well as motivate individuals. But unfortunately, many CEOs developed their careers with a belief in individual accomplishment and traditional hierarchies. They are at a serious disadvantage when they need to deliver results through a team or to organize the business along team lines.

People who work in teams bring two main aspects of themselves to the team. The first is their technical skill; the second is their personal skill as a team player. Dr Meredith Belbin (*Team Roles at Work,* Butterworth- Heinemann, 1993) developed a simple team theory which asserts that all good teams need a mixture of different team skills. These are:

> **A CEO must select a team which reflects his needs more than his prejudices.**

- Schedulers (list makers)
- Co-ordinators (chairmen)
- Shapers (task-oriented people)
- Creative ideas people
- Ideas researchers (resources investigators)
- Team workers (team feelings specialists)
- Objective judges
- Completer finishers (check the job gets completed).

An individual manager may excel at one of these team skills. He may be proficient at a second. But he will rarely excel in more than two. A CEO must select a team which reflects his needs more than his prejudices.

The "overendowed" intellectual

I worked for many years with a bright and extremely intellectual leader. We first became acquainted when I was his tutor in strategy on a managing directors' program that he was attending.

We had evidence that this man had a large capacity for intellectual analysis of most business problems, but he did not seem to relate at a human level to his subordinates at work. This doubt was recorded and explained why his promotion to managing director status came several years later than expected.

When he had been in the post about a year he telephoned to tell me his board of directors were not really knitting together as a team. Could I help? By the time he called me in, he had already changed most members of his team. He had a new marketing director, a new information technology director and was about to appoint a fresh finance director.

I asked him what criteria he had used to compose his team. He responded: "They are a thoroughly intellectual group of people. Every one of them has a high IQ." I pointed out that he, as MD, had enough brain power and IQ for any team. What he needed from his people was empathy and emotional insight into the feelings of the company and its customers. He agreed – but it was too late; the new people were in position.

A year later he and his board decided to change the company's technology. It was an intellectually daring and exciting challenge. The change went catastrophically wrong when the workers in the company proved unable to change their work habits. The company started to lose money at the rate of 10 percent of total revenue. He and his board were all asked to leave the company.

As managers climb higher in an organization, they need to become increasingly conceptual in their thinking and leadership style. The problems they have to solve are less technical and more conceptual. They are employed to make judgments and select solutions from many different ways of achieving the purposes of the organization. The solutions are never simply "right" or "wrong." Solutions are made successful by the determination shown by leaders in making them work.

For example, should the organization stick to its core skills or diversify? Should there be a divisional structure based on geography, products, or functions? There are no right answers to these questions. Leaders have to make choices from equally valid, largely incomparable solutions. Their leadership and management skills are tested when they have to turn their personal belief into a practical

> *As managers climb higher in an organization, they need to become increasingly conceptual in their thinking and leadership style.*

solution that everybody in the organization believes in. That is when the CEO or MD needs a certain level of "charisma" to ensure effectiveness. Charisma must be used to convince subordinates that one's policies, strategies, or solutions will work – leaders need sufficient "personality" to convince people the solutions they believe in are right for the organization's future.

Charisma-bypass syndrome

Some leaders simply do not possess sufficient charisma (sometimes known as charisma-bypass syndrome). The symptoms of the syndrome are quite clear. The leader is boring and regularly fails to inspire his people to follow his lead. People fall asleep in his meetings. Even if they bring large mugs of coffee with them when going for their annual appraisal with a charisma-bypass leader or manager – the coffee doesn't help. People with the syndrome seem to create narcolepsy wherever they visit. The effect upon the organization can be dreadful. Leaders suffering from this syndrome can make any job, for any and every subordinate, the dullest on earth. There are no known cures, vaccines, or occurrences of remission from this terrible affliction.

These are the subtle and difficult ultimate tradeoffs that only the CEO or chairman have to make. It explains why more promotion mistakes are made at that level of appointment than any other in the organization.

3 Problems of executives reporting to the CEO

There is a special tension attached to the role of executives reporting to the CEO. Usually at least one of those reporting is a "director of finance." This role carries the added burden of a legal responsibility to report the finances and accounts of the organization in a manner which conforms to legislation. This can be used to exercise power but it may also be a source of stress when it is necessary to enforce rules against the wishes of the CEO or chairperson who is nominally in charge of him.

Further considerations apply to others reporting to the CEO. Depending upon the structure of the organization, these executives may be managing directors of divisions of the business or leaders of functions such as marketing, sales, information technology, human resources, or manufacturing.

One often finds that executives reporting to the CEO have a strong tendency to "run their own show." They are usually in charge of substantial parts of the business and want to retain the maximum independence. The role of the CEO is to allow them the maximum freedom within the constraint of ensuring they do not actually damage the interests of the overall organization. This is a different concept to the stakeholder theory referred to above. The concepts are known as *integration and differentiation* and were first developed by Lawrence and Lorsch of Harvard University and are written up in their seminal work, *Managing Integration and Differentiation* (Harvard University Press, 1967).

> **Different functions within the firm have a natural tendency to compete with other functions unless the way they are instructed to carry out their responsibilities is carefully co-ordinated.**

They observed that different functions within businesses have a natural tendency to compete with other functions unless the way they are instructed to carry out their responsibilities is carefully co-ordinated. For example, a manufacturing director may want to reduce the number of changes to a production run and will usually prefer to make as small a range of different sizes as possible, to keep costs under control. The marketing or sales director will want as large a range of sizes and colors as possible in order to maximize the range to enable his salespeople to sell more. Such contradictions are defined by Lawrence and Lorsch as the "differentiation" tendency. The need for integration is provided by the CEO or chairman who must reconcile these differentiating tendencies to ensure the optimal balance of cost, price, and variety in the general interests of the organization.

The key role of senior executives is to deliver promises to the CEO about budgets, plans, and profits. Any senior executive who cannot commit to the necessary promises should not be allowed to remain at a senior level for long. Although a senior executive deserves and needs time to adapt to his position, he also needs the ability to "hit the ground running," i.e. to deliver results even while he is still learning the job.

Executives often complain that they cannot be judged on one year's performance when the investment decisions they take have two or three-year payoff periods. The main counter argument to these assertions is that the right to have two and three-year investments comes from delivery of the one-year targets!

The essential fabric of any organization
is based on loyalty

There is one absolute rule for all organizational life. Behavior in organizations must be based upon loyalty, to both the organization and one's colleagues. Managers invariably demand it of their subordinates while sometimes failing to give it to their own superior. Any display of disloyalty will be instantly picked up by a team. Managers may think that their subordinates will not notice the odd disparaging disloyal phrase about their own boss. Often it is only to let out a passing moment of anger. It will not pass unnoticed. Once a manager sows the organizational seed of disloyalty, it will return to haunt him and may well destroy him when he most needs loyalty from his own subordinates.

Loyalty does not mean that one never criticizes aspects of the firm's way of conducting its business. Nor does it mean always accepting the behavior or plans of the boss. It should mean that, when criticism is necessary, it is constructive. If it is respectfully heard – but rejected – the debate is over. One must then decide whether the issue is big enough to be worth a resignation. If it is not, whether the manager has won or lost, loyalty means one accepts the decision, stands by it and *loyally* communicates it, without comment.

Being loyal to the organization cannot preclude "whistle blowing." If your organization has committed unethical or immoral acts, whether in its sales methods, the quality of its products, the way it handles after-sales service, or the way it treats its employees, there is always a higher level of loyalty to oneself and one's own ethical standards. One cannot automatically assume that the organization is wrong when measured by one person's personal standards. However, after careful consideration, if one feels the organization is breaking important social or personal moral standards, one should place the public interest before that of the organization and reveal the truth.

It is difficult for those that stay in an organization which "has been whistle blown." Often the leader (if they are responsible for what is wrong) continues to insist that they are right and the whistle blower wrong. The people around them get asked to support vindictive, irrational behavior against the whistle blower. It is at times like these that your moral fiber will be tested to the maximum.

The abnormal psychologies of senior managers

Managers achieve organizational objectives by getting other people to do tasks to achieve the objectives. Many people find the task of managing people to get things done rather than doing tasks oneself, to be counter-intuitive behavior. It takes a special kind of psychology to want to earn a living getting other people to do things – and to be measured by the results of their concerted efforts.

> It takes a special kind of psychology to want to earn a living getting other people to do things.

Furthermore, as managers climb the hierarchy of their organizations, one notices certain types of character and personality emerging. They seem to share some similarities and values.

For many years I have used psychometric tests as a tool to help me understand the individuals I am working with. My preferred test is the FIRO-B which stands for Fundamental Interpersonal Relations, Orientations-Behavior.

It measures several aspects of a manager's behaviour:

1 How often he expresses a need to be included in groups.
2 How much inclusion he really wants (in contrast to how much he expresses).
3 How much control he likes to assert over others.
4 How much control he can accept from others.
5 How much affection he expresses toward others.
6 How much affection he wants from others.
7 How much anger or frustration he expresses or suppresses.
8 How much he prefers his own company, compared to preferring to be with other people.

My findings on the behavior of senior managers are startling.

Inclusion – the "social skill"

Most managers develop the necessary interpersonal skills to *express inclusion*. This is a social or managerial skill. This skill enables them to create the impression of being a team person. However, when we look at how much *inclusion they really desire*, we find that often they do not really want it at all. In other words, they indicate inclusiveness through their language and behavior to their subordinates but the evidence from the tests conducted demonstrates they do not actually enjoy it. This may make their behavior appear hypocritical to their subordinates. It could be characterized as "always ensuring themselves an invitation to the Christmas party but never turning up."

The manager's need to control

There is a similar pattern of contrasts between the results for *control wanted* compared with *control accepted*. Most senior executives taking this test enjoy *controlling others* but do not like *accepting control from others*. Again, this will be seen as two incompatible behaviors by their subordinates (as well as by their superiors who have the same problem, but often do not recognize it). Subordinates understand that their boss expects compliance from them. They then observe his reluctance to comply with the control needs of his own boss. This need to control others while avoiding control oneself may explain much about the rise to the top of many senior managers. This drive is probably at least as important as business skill or talent.

Affection – the warm center nobody feels

Finally, there appears to be a less strong – but still real – contrast between the amount of *affection wanted* compared to the *amount of affection expressed to others* by senior managers. Senior executives measured on the FIRO-B test seem to want more affection than the affection they are able to express to others. My research shows that they display little affection at work. They may warm up when they arrive home, but not much. Their behavior will resemble more the caricature of the executive who arrives home from the office and says: "Hello, I'm home. It's been a terrible day. Where's my supper and why haven't you told me yet that you love me?"

Anger and frustration

The test also gives a measure of the anger or frustration felt by the respondent. In general this is evenly distributed between high, medium, and low. However, it is worth noting that both low and high anger or frustration indicators can cause problems for subordinates. People who do not show their anger or frustration can be very difficult to work for because they do not give enough signals to their subordinates about their feelings.

For example, when they are not satisfied with the subordinate's quality of work they tend to suppress their anger or frustration and fail to tell the employee of their dissatisfaction. When, eventually, they call the employee to the office to tell him he is being dismissed because he has been under-performing, the employee will be totally surprised. The worst aspect of low-anger-expression people is that they may fail in their key management role to coach their subordinates to improve their performance.

The excessively passive boss

A chief executive I worked with had a very low anger level. He had a managing director working for him who was performing poorly and who, unfortunately, had a very high anger score. This combination set them both up for a catastrophe.

The CEO took the MD out to dinner to explain that he wanted him to improve his management performance. Failing some improvement, he (the CEO) would have to dismiss him. The following day the CEO wrote to the MD to confirm the points he thought he had made clearly. The MD wrote back an angry letter denying that the CEO had explained anything of the sort. He rejected any of the criticism implied in the letter.

What had happened was that the low-anger-threshold CEO just did not know how to express anger. The CEO had spent weeks steeling himself to really lay it on the line for his rebellious subordinate and spell out in no uncertain terms what was wrong and needed to be put right. He did not think that he needed to scream and shout to get his points across.

The MD had the opposite problem. Because anger was his basic mode of self-expression, when he heard the CEO expressing what was wrong quietly and impassively, he assumed that it was just ordinary evening dinner conversation, not worth taking special note of.

The two of them never did learn to communicate. Not long afterward, the CEO had to ask the MD to leave. The CEO never learned how to express himself when dissatisfied with a subordinate's poor performance, and the MD never learned to control his anger.

High anger levels can be equally dangerous. If a senior manager quickly displays high levels of frustration or anger, they will rapidly find people unwilling to come to meetings to discuss anything at all. Most people avoid angry bosses – they are too unpredictable and make people feel endangered. One high anger boss I worked with scored 100 out of 100 for his anger scale. When I told him he said "That explains a lot. I run an open door policy in my office – but do you think I can ever get anybody to come through that door?"

The findings from these psychometric tests are important. They demonstrate that senior executives may have attitudes about inclusion, affection, and control which differ from normal populations. This, in turn, causes distortions in their management style. These abnormal behaviors become the exemplars for the managers who are learning from them.

These results show there may be built-in resistances from senior executives toward concepts of teamwork. When so many senior executives prefer to control others and avoid being controlled themselves, there is a real problem for the organization's capacity for teamwork. Complex organizations need people to be capable of both giving and receiving control at every level in the organization. Managers who need to control and cannot accept control are intrinsically and psychologically unsuited to the teamwork required in many modern corporations' complex structures.

Conclusions

It is difficult to be a senior manager or a leader. Sometimes this is because leaders forget how difficult it is to be a follower. Most people who get to the top did not do it only by design. They are often naturally gifted people who also had the good sense, judgment and good fortune to avoid the wide range of catastrophes waiting along the road of every career.

This chapter has tried to offer warning signals to managers about the potential traps along the path to the top. Formulating strategy at the highest level of conceptual power has to be carried out at the top of an organization. There are many structural reasons why senior leaders get it wrong. However, some of the dangers can be avoided if they have both the talent and humility to heed the warning signals. Leadership and management are vitally important roles in society and commerce. Heeding the symptoms when things are going wrong as well as constantly trying to learn from the mistakes of the past, are the minimum safeguards that should be heeded to try and get it right.

Additional reading for this chapter

M. Belbin, *Management Team – Why They Succeed or Fail*, Butterworth-Heinemann, Oxford, 1991

G. Hamel and C. K. Pralahad, *Competing for the Future*, Harvard Business School Press, Boston, 1994

C. Levicki, *The Leadership Gene*, Financial Times Pitman Publishing, London, 1998

S. Slatter, *Corporate Recovery*, Penguin, Harmondsworth, Middlesex, 1984

Getting Implementation Right

Why strategy implementation needs great leadership as well as organization of the firm's resources

The relationship between strategy and communication

How a strong team is vital for strategy implementation

Advice on becoming a great leader

Final words on hubris, luck, and communications

In this chapter I want to tell you what I have learned about how to get strategy implementation right.

> *"The important thing is not to stop questioning."*
>
> Albert Einstein

The formula for success

Strategy implementation can be reduced to the following thesis which covers every successful strategy enactment I have studied. It is easy to write down but hard to do.

Successful strategy implementation requires: great leadership. which is defined by – vision, focus, communication skills, and profound determination – all reinforced by moral fiber.

Furthermore, there has to be a synergy between the core competencies of the organization, its strategy and structure, the desires of the stakeholders – and then you need a little luck.

The practicalities of implementation

1 Communicating the mission and the strategy

This workout has shown how to ensure that one includes all the vital stages of analysis which must be taken into account before deciding the long-term mission and strategy for your organization. The previous chapter described how many leaders get it wrong. In this chapter I want to tell you what I have learned about how to get strategy implementation right.

Communication and dissemination of the strategy to *every part* of the organization is the prime requirement. This really does mean everybody. The way your front-line people treat your customers is probably a key factor in how your customers form impressions about your business. If your company is in the hotel industry, your doorman and then the reception staff are in the front-line of customer perception management. Do they know the values you espouse? Do you keep loading your staff with extra tasks which means they are never quite ready to look after customers when they arrive, hot and flustered, from whatever journey they have just completed? If you manufacture car components, does your mission tell your employees the business must be a "fault-free zone"? If you are in a food business, does the strategy proclaim hygiene in every sentence?

The mission and the strategy of your business should tell everybody the key values directly. Otherwise your employees can only rely on the accidental signals around them. By the way, if you do not guide employees on the purposes of the organization, it should come as no surprise when entirely extraneous incidents change their attitudes, e.g. your hotel doorman frowns when it snows and smiles when the sun shines.

2 Subdividing the mission and vision

The most difficult task for a leader is to subdivide the total strategic direction into manageable parts for each of the executives, managers, and other employees to implement. The leadership may have a vision of what the business will look like in ten years' time; they might want the business to go from national to international; from low technology to high technology with the installation of computers and standard services to clients (e.g. banks and similar financial institutions over the past 10 to 20 years); from being a specific supplier of a particular food to a supplier of a general menu (e.g. McDonald's used to sell only hamburgers, now it sells chicken, pizza, and fish products).

How should the leader subdivide the strategic vision of what the changed organization will look like in ten years' time? One cannot expect subordinates to know what action to take to implement that vision. It is the responsibility of strategic leadership to allocate tasks to each executive, manager, and staff member to ensure that they understand what has to be done to make the mission and strategic objectives happen. That does not mean that the leader writes the job description for every person in the firm. But he must allocate all aspects of the mission and strategy to each of his subordinates to ensure that they understand what they must do. It is the subordinate's role, if competent, to further break it into smaller tasks for his own team members, and so on throughout the business.

For example, if it is the mission of Boeing, the US aircraft manufacturer, to achieve a 50 percent share of all civil aircraft supply to airlines throughout the world within (say) 15 years, then the executive president might divide that task up respectively amongst his senior vice-presidents for finance, operations, research and development (R&D), human resources, marketing, and production. To the operations officer he may say: "I will judge you over the next five years if you manage to capture 30 percent of the world market, because that gives me hope that we can achieve the 50 percent within 15 years." He may say to his marketing manager, "I will judge you within three years if you have achieved an order book which shows the potential for 23 percent of world sales because that gives us a chance of delivering my 30 percent to the president in five years, and the 50 percent he wants in 15 years." To his research and development senior vice-president he will probably say, "I want drawings and plans for three civil aircraft that can capture the long-haul, short-hop, and private fleet markets that carry more passengers per mile at a cheaper rate by a margin of 15 percent than any other competing aircraft available from any of our competitors in the world. I expect those plans to be so exciting that our order book, at least on tentative orders, will show a potential of 45 percent and a probability, after cancellation, of 25 percent within three years." To his senior vice-   president for production he might say, "I want to see working drawings on those planes that make it look probable that at least two of the three can be built in the time frame envisaged and meet exactly the specification and promises our marketing department is making to the customers."

The point of this example is that no particular subordinate is responsible for achieving the overall strategy. That is the leader's role. The achievement by each subordinate of his part of the strategy will deliver the overall strategy in the time frame envisaged.

3 Examine and test your team

The point about the example is that the leader's role in subdividing the strategic objectives is effected when each subordinate is given a set of tasks that he or she feels capable of achieving. The reason he or she feels capable of achieving it will be based partly on that individual's own self-beliefs. It will be equally based upon the leader's skills in communicating to the individual *his belief that he or she can do it* and that the leader, with the subordinate, fully intends to achieve the objectives. Inspiring people with the belief that things can be done is a key skill of leadership. The underlying psychological skill is to understand how the minds of each of your subordinates works. Leaders need to know when subordinates are fearful and how to make them feel courageous. What kind of task can they accomplish easily?

> *The leader's role in subdividing the strategic objectives is effected when each subordinate is given a set of tasks that he or she feels capable of achieving.*

When do they need special, motivating reinforcement to make them believe they can do it? Your belief in them is part of their belief in themselves. They must perceive it as unfaltering, unwavering, and absolute. It should never be the leader's demotivating lack of belief in somebody that causes the person to fail.

You also have the duty of regularly examining the basis for your belief in each individual in your team. One has to continuously consider whether the team members are working beyond the limits of their skills. Just when do they become strained because they do not have the conceptual power or intelligence to carry out the next difficult task or role? If you recognize that anybody is reaching that point, you may need to share your feelings with that person. This is the moment when your greatest wisdom as a leader can manifest itself. How? The person who is not performing at this level, spent many years getting to this position and has probably given sterling value to the organization and has made profits for it. It is not a good idea for such a person to leave the organization. A wise leader will find another job within the organization that he or she can accept with dignity and which uses all his or her accumulated know-how and experience for the continued good of the organization. It might also be wise to check one's own decision and be sure that it is not the decision which is at fault, rather than the executive.

Two wise men

The best example I have seen of this phenomenon of refusing to lose long accumulated expertise occurred in a large transport concern. The chairman appointed a subordinate from a managing director's role to a main board position in charge of a highly troubled division.

It was obvious within a year that this appointment was not going to be successful. The new board member had little strategic vision and was incapable of leading the business he had been allocated.

The chairman went to see him and they agreed that he should go back to being the successful managing director of just one of the businesses instead of the unsuccessful leader of all of them. As a wise and mature man, he recognized the chairman's wisdom and accepted the demotion. (It was softened by him being allowed to retain some of the privileges of the main board reward package.)

For many years thereafter the subordinate made many more millions of pounds of profit for his employer, doing a job he knew well. He inspired many other people to go past him and on to higher levels than himself. The chairman's wisdom in retaining that man had earned the chairman his salary many times over.

When examining your team's "fitness" to implement the agreed strategy, it may sometimes be useful to employ outside help to analyze and judge whether team members are up to the mark. Over many years I have been asked to do this kind of task. Although one has to be highly ethical in making judgments about people, one does develop instinct and insight about the necessary skill levels for senior board positions. I also recommend the selective use of psychometric tests and other analytical human resource tools. They should never be the only criteria for judgment – but they can help. Some (such as the Belwin Team Test and the FIRO-B) are particularly useful in discovering why a group of bright people who, in theory, ought to make a perfect team, just do not seem to knit and work well together.

4 Judge on the future, not the past

When one reflects on whether one has the right team to make the strategy happen, it is important not to judge the team on its past achievements, but on the tasks and jobs you have in mind for the future of the organization. This is difficult but necessary. Too many people keep their jobs at senior level because the leader keeps referring back to how good they were when they ran a $40 million revenue business or a $500 million revenue business. However, if the objective in the future is for them to run their $2 billion segment of the business, then the past is not a predictor of the future. The harsh reality to be judged is whether they are showing evidence of success on the $2 billion job rather than the smaller job which they successfully pursued in the past. That was the reason they were promoted to the new job. It should not be the reason why you *keep* them in the new job. That should relate only to future performance. This phenomenon of retaining excessive respect for past performance, rather than capacity for future achievement, explains why far too many people are kept too long in the wrong job, at levels beyond their competence, by chairmen who are making their judgment based on the past, rather than the future needs of the organization.

This is not to suggest that one should not respect past achievements or look after employees who have given sterling service but have now become worn out. I certainly believe they should be looked after. That behavior forms part of the moral fiber and culture of the organization. But they should not be allowed to block the future because the organization owes them respect for the past. That respect can be paid in other ways which do not destroy the customers' expectations, the futures of the younger employees, and the wealth of the business's investors.

Basic criteria of skills

There are three measures which are relevant to the basic analysis of people's potential. They run in the following order of importance:

1 Loyalty
2 Intelligence
3 Enthusiasm.

The loyalty test is the absolute "litmus test" of fitness for team membership. If there is any possibility of disloyalty to the leader, the organization, the strategy, the mission, or the organization's values, then the executive must be counseled, allowed time to change, and retested at an early date. Disloyalty cannot be contemplated from any member of a team which is asked to deliver an important strategic mission. It is the corporate equivalent of biological cancer.

The second test is of intelligence. This does not mean that subordinates need to have a high IQ. It means they have to understand with some form of brain power what the leader is trying to do. This may be intuitive or deductive. It could be with a slow brain or a fast one. Whatever brain processing system they use, they have to show that they understand the strategy sufficiently well to translate it into appropriate time spans of achievement for their subordinates. I emphasize that this does *not* require a high IQ, but it does require some form of understanding. If they cannot show basic understanding of the key

Disloyalty cannot be contemplated from any member of a team which is asked to deliver an important strategic mission.

strategic messages, then they cannot possibly translate it for their people to achieve.

However, if they have at least the insight, coupled with the third ingredient of *enthusiasm* to achieve the task, then they can probably deliver the strategic objectives needed from them. The capacity to instill enthusiasm in people around and below them with the desire to deliver and a determination to succeed is a golden quality that should be valued, treasured, and embraced.

The marketing man

I was asked by the leader of a large organization, with a revenue of £2 billion, to assess his marketing director. The MD believed the latter was making no contribution because the organization had grown too large for the marketer to cope with.

The marketing director was a delightful and utterly charming man. I was determined to do everything I could to save him. I explained his superior's frustration to him and told him to prepare a strategic marketing plan with the key elements the MD had devised for the future of the organization. I urged him to fax it to me as soon as possible.

Four weeks later I saw the boss and he asked me again whether he ought to dismiss the marketing manager. I was surprised that he had not received the strategic marketing documents from the marketer (but then, neither had I).

I went to see the marketing director and asked what had happened. He explained that he had been sidetracked. I explained that he was being sidetracked from saving his job! He asked for a weekend to prepare the documents. When I received them they were poor – but they could be made into a reasonable document. They mainly lacked, however, the underlying principles of the organization and their application to the marketing role. I explained this and asked him to just make those primary additions to the front of the text before putting it in front of the boss.

Two days later he telephoned me to explain he did not really understand what we were talking about. He could neither conceptualize the principles nor translate them into marketing terms.

The good news was that he was not dismissed. We discovered that everybody else liked him too. He was given a role in personnel and happily "helps" people all day, as personnel people do.

Audit the skills of the rest of the workforce

Core competencies were described earlier in this book (Chapter 2). The strategic implementation team must assess whether the organization has the right mix of core competencies to deliver its strategic objectives. For example, if one wanted to reduce people-based administration to an IT-led process system (as did the banks mentioned earlier), then one has to acquire competencies in information technology and technology processing to deliver that part of the strategic intent. The organization will also need human resource skills to reduce the workforce when people are supplanted by the technology. These are special skills and it is unlikely they will be sitting around in the organization waiting to be exploited. They will have to be acquired, either from competitors or by developing them in-house.

That is not a simple decision. The competencies may not be easily available in the open marketplace. The organization's need may be such an innovative use of the technology that the whole process has to be custom built from start to finish. One could buy in the service from an external supplier (e.g. EDS is a global information technology processing organization supplying those needs to organizations around the world, usually as an insider within the organization).

When auditing the workforce one also has to understand what new skills, both technical and managerial, will be required as a result of the new or changed strategic objectives. Have your people been properly developed in the past? Does the organization need just a modification of training and development? Or do you need a new and total organization-wide, development program? You may decide to develop special relationships with business schools or a particular consultancy organization which will invest in learning about your organization and, therefore, give you better value for money. Hopping around between suppliers can be an expensive game as you pay for each of them to go up the learning curve to understand your unique organization, and the particular training needs of your people.

The structure of the organization

If you have decided to make substantial changes to the strategic purpose and objectives of the organization, you will have to reexamine the organization's structure to decide whether it fits the new needs. Will the old structure carry the new strategy or must it be changed?

The clear principle of structural change, as I have indicated in previous chapters, is to make as few modifications as possible. It has become fashionable for leaders to promise continuous change. I believe nothing can be more calculated to completely demotivate the workforce than that kind of utterly misguided statement.

The speed of change is getting faster. Technology and innovation have shorter life cycles than they used to have. However, even though external circumstances have changed, the nature of human beings, formed over millennia, has not changed to match. Human beings enjoy stability. They have strong hopes that tomorrow will be similar to today. People like to work in organizations where they understand what opportunities exist and where they see how they might move up the ladder of achievement to maximize the use of their skills and the limits of their ambition. Every time an organization is restructured, many of the rules of the game are changed. This leaves people ignorant about their future and fearful for their careers.

> *If you have decided to make substantial changes to the strategic purpose and objectives of the organization, you will have to reexamine the organization's structure to decide whether it fits the new needs.*

But if one has to restructure?

However, although it is our most forceful possible advice that you make as few changes to the structure of the organization as possible, how do you proceed when you have to restructure? It is a useful primary first principle to find any way you can to make the necessary changes without large-scale announcements either of redundancies or new positions and titles for your people. The basic rule is: *Say as little as possible and write even less.* This rule makes it much easier to move people into new positions and different responsibilities than when you proclaim that sweeping changes are going to be necessary. That merely puts everybody into a state of fear and also induces a "politicization" of most managers' behavior. Equally invidious is the publication of formal organizational charts, showing definitively who appears to be a winner, and, therefore, how many people are losers as a result of the changes. When you formalize the restructuring, you often generate far more demotivation than enthusiasm.

Evolution always beats revolution

Another reason for making changes as imperceptibly as possible over time, rather than instantaneously, is that the best structures are those that evolve as new needs become apparent.

It is not always easy, at the beginning of a long strategic journey, to know exactly what structures will be appropriate. Let them evolve as the need for new core competencies or different business directions emerge (whether geographical, intellectual, technological, human, or capital). It is far better to wait and see than try to guess them all in advance.

Finally, another basic rule about structure is not to tell your competitors. Intelligent competitors will use knowledge about your organization's structure to predict your strategic intentions. If the strategic intent is worth having, it is worth keeping to yourself and your workforce. Naturally, you cannot stop some people leaving and joining the competitors. Hopefully, you will always retain your key people. Those who understand most, at the very top of the ladder, would be wise to remain discreet in order to preserve their own reputations for integrity. Ultimately, no single person, or even group of people, can walk away from the company with all the strategic objectives, and its enthusiasm to win and capacity to succeed. The potential success belongs to the organization and no single group of people should have total ownership.

For example, when the UK Government deregulated the banks in the City of London in the mid-1980s, many banking businesses tried to capture teams with special expertise from rival banks. Most of those transfers did not work because small groups and teams rarely represent the whole organization. The organization's ethos and strength is based on its past achievements and its future intentions. If any one team is able to transport them all to a competitor, then something is wrong with the strategic intent or with the organization's vulnerability and risk management.

How can you become a great leader?

Although many assume leaders are "born," some aspects of leadership can be learned. A first guideline to becoming a great leader is to be ruthlessly honest with yourself, particularly as you reach the higher echelons of the organization. Have you become one of those vainglorious and arrogant people you used to disdain when you were seeking promotion in the organization? Do you mainly talk *at*, rather than *to*, people? Do you talk more than you listen? Do you enjoy visiting different parts of the organization or do you run your role from a desk in an ivory tower with just accounts and rumors as your decision tools? Are you investing in yourself to learn how to become more charismatic? Are you persuading people that your strategic purposes are rational and well thought through? Have you convinced them that the very best thing for the organization and for their personal futures is your strategy? Or do you just tell them what to do and expect it to happen?

Many leaders find it useful to have a mentor. It is strange that, although one finds many leaders subscribe to the concept of acting as mentors to their subordinates, they have not realized that mentors for leaders are equally valuable! The idea of mentoring within organizations is to ensure that particularly promising people have somebody at a senior level in the organization guiding their careers, to ensure they get chances to develop those careers. It is especially useful for women, who frequently meet male chauvinism which blocks their career progression. Mentors can also sometimes protect individuals from the enemies that successful people accumulate because they threaten less talented managers who consider themselves equally deserving. It is strange that few leaders realize that if you need mentors as you go up the ladder, you just as surely need them when you are at the top. The loneliest jobs in the world are those of chairman, president, chief executive, chief operating officer, or managing director in any small, medium, or large organization. You cannot talk to subordinates about your fears and inhibitions. It is not easy to trust people around you because when you admit your weakness to them you may also be removing their belief in and enthusiasm for your leadership. You may well need a mentor outside the organization. It is highly advisable that you find a friend whom you can trust. By the way, although a husband or wife is often thought of as being the best mentor, it is equally important to find a business friend who can offer more insight and business understanding than the pure sympathy of a listening ear.

Continuous improvement

Many leaders get to the top of the organization with a belief that they have learned everything and are now employed only to apply their skills. Evidence shows you can never know everything and you should never stop learning. It is vital to continue to train oneself and remember that new skills and understanding are required every day. Ask young graduate employees, who have just obtained their university degrees, what the latest developments in technology, biology, or computer science are. Go to research laboratories and find out what new research is taking place. (You may also find out that they do not understand your strategic purpose. How can they conduct research for the organization if they do not know about its strategic future?) Investigate the latest hopes and enthusiasms of youth. Young people are the tomorrow the organization is working for.

Take time out to go on personal development programs at the best business schools. Find out there, from people with similar jobs, how they are approaching it. They probably share the same doubts and concerns as yourself. You can learn from their ideas about how to become a better leader with your particular skills, personality, intelligence, and strategic insight. The objective always is to make yourself a better quality individual who can make strategy happen for your organization.

Stay in touch with all your stakeholders

Many potentially great leaders fail to deliver their vision when they reach the top of the organization, because they have not understood the need to stay in touch with all of the stakeholders – it is especially important to retain the ability to carry their Board to back their necessary decisions.

One chairman of a $20 billion business for which I acted as a consultant runs the whole of his diary based on his analysis of stakeholder importance. That is to say, he devises with his assistants, the correct time priorities to be allocated to each of the important stakeholders whose interests he must balance. Every three months he audits his diary with his personal team to check that he has actually used his time in accordance with the importance of the stakeholders. They also reassess whether their original balance of importance of those stakeholders needs to be changed. Using this method, he has been known to refuse a meeting with an assistant to the President of the United States because it did not rate at the correct level on the stakeholder analysis. I am not suggesting that he has necessarily got it totally right, but it is an extreme example of remembering to look after your stakeholders.

Another exceptionally gifted executive I worked with for many years was predicted to become the executive vice-president of his corporation. I always used to tell him to invest in spending more time with the non-executive officers of his business. He responded that he believed his business record would speak for itself and he was more interested in making profits for the corporation than developing political skills and techniques. Unfortunately, he only realized why he should have invested in building relationships with those important stakeholders when he did not get the top job that he had spent 25 years trying to achieve. The incumbent chairman did not like him and brought in an outsider above him, a person who had none of his business skills. That person eventually halved the value of the shareholders' stock. Sadly though, it was too late for the other leader.

Communications

Once you have decided upon the strategic direction of your organization, you must communicate it. The larger the organization, the more time you need to devote to communicating with everybody in it. You can never communicate too much. That does not mean you have the right to be boring because that will defeat your purposes. You will have to think continuously of new ways to communi-

> *Once you have decided upon the strategic direction of your organization, you must communicate it.*

cate the same messages about the standards, rules, values, behavior, and tasks to your people all the time.

When you visit a company site, they will notice if you speak to a secretary or pick up a piece of scrap paper from the floor because you care about the site being tidy. If you pass one of your operating teams digging a hole in the road and stop to talk to them about the job they are doing and also, tell them about your hopes for the company and for their future, it will travel along the informal grapevine of the organization in hours, with a rapidity that is beyond belief. Everything a great leader does gets translated into: "the way we do things around here." This also places an onerous burden upon you. Every time you have a violent argument with a subordinate, he will "learn" that bad temper and rudeness is permissible. Whenever you deal harshly or unjustly with somebody who has to leave the organization, it will be seen as a less caring place.

Alternatively, whenever you act kindly to somebody whose wife is sick in hospital or whose husband has had an accident at his place of employment, the unfortunate person's colleagues will know that your organization is merciful, gentle, and kind. It is possible that in your private life you believe that good deeds are done silently. This may well not apply in terms of good deeds in the organization. There is an organizational rationale to this. If you are spending organizational resources to carry out your act of kindness, then the organization has a right to benefit from it. This is particularly so if you are behaving kindly because it is also meant to demonstrate a value system about people and that this is the value you wish to instill in them. When spending organizational resources you have *no* right to false modesty. You are obliged to use it or allow it to be known that the kind act is an exemplification of the company's belief in kindness.

The value of stability

It is important not to change standards and beliefs frequently. One should never change rules relating to honesty and ethics, unless you have discovered a weakness and want to improve the standards. I particularly want to emphasize the word *ethics* as we begin to close this book. It is vital that you take the trouble to understand what you truly believe. Those beliefs should be based, as far as possible, upon eternal standards, values, and moral concepts. In my experience, if you do not do it consciously, your behavior will still be seen in ethical terms – but the effect will be a series of accidents.

Over the years I have learned that all people have a right to take their ethics to work with them. I have met many religious, devout, and pious people who thought they had to leave their moral precepts and the values which dominate their private lives at home. I have always asserted, and, hopefully frequently persuaded many of them, that this is a wrong approach. If you are leading a high-quality, moral, personal life you have both a right and a duty to take those morals and values to work with you. If those values work in your private life, there is no reason to believe that they will not be equally efficacious at work.

I do not intend here to suggest that leaders have a right to force their personal moral codes upon their employees. They have to couch their value systems in terms that persuade people they are right for the business. People must be happy to behave in the moral way their leaders want when they are working for the organization. If the leader's or the organization's "way of doing things' conflicts too strongly with the personal views of too many employees, they will soon find they have no staff to do the work.

People around you deserve and need the inspiration of the high values with which you live your private life. You will inspire them to manage and create a better quality organization.

Under most circumstances, profits can be achieved while also behaving properly and decently. As we move into a new millennium, it is vital that people take the moral high ground and enact high quality beliefs in their private and public lives. What I am offering here is a entirely personal view. There is always the risk that some of you reading this book are thoroughly immoral and unethical people. If you are, the only comment one could possibly make, is that one hopes you fail – and as soon as possible. The danger of unethical people leading organizations is that they taint the organization itself and every human being in it. Most organizations do not

> *Under most circumstances, profits can be achieved while also behaving properly and decently.*

exist to do good but to make profits (this may not apply to some charitable institutions). Nevertheless, profits should never be achieved at the cost of doing harm to society or individuals. Under most circumstances, profits can be achieved while also behaving properly and decently.

It is also appropriate to say that there may be some businesses which cannot possibly do good. I speak here of organizations which exist to sell drugs or addiction-inducing products. I sincerely believe, that in the fullness of civilized time, such organizations will self-destruct or public opinion will no longer allow them to exist.

Doubts and fears

As the strategic leader of your organization, you should have doubts and fears. If you do not, then you are probably a menace. Doubt and fear are the tools which give you the adrenalin to overcome your problems and succeed. You should understand that people around you, while often appearing confident, are also fearful, intimidated, and frightened by the enormity of the tasks they have to deliver. They are frightened by the difficult budgets imposed by their leaders and by the complexity of an external environment that is turbulent and difficult. Do not be shy of using your own fear. It is important to understand that it is shared by many people who often give no hint that they are also fearful.

Beware hubris

Your fears and doubts are also important for another vital purpose. You can use them to retain your modesty and humility. These are key ingredients of great leaders. They form a contraceptive against *hubris*. Hubris describes the vainglorious or excessive pride in themselves that some leaders develop on moving up the corporate ladder. If disloyalty is a corporate cancer then hubris is a personal, managerial one. Arrogance, excessive self-belief, failure to admit doubt or fear, can have appalling consequences for your organization. That is how hubris creeps up on you. One often thinks of Richard Nixon as the ultimate example of hubris and its effect upon moral fiber. No matter how high one climbs, it always means that, ultimately, you have further to fall. At the end of the day, all your human achievements are measured by human standards. Organizations go on long after individuals have departed and are always bigger than even apparently brilliant individuals. Retain your humility – its loss could be damaging to your health.

How to be lucky

In some ways the oldest clichés are the best. All the lucky people seem to work hard. Working long hours does not mean "working long hours at the expense of a private life." Long hours at work should be a function of total energy capacity. Some people are lucky enough to have waking hours of 18 out of 24. Others need to sleep 10 hours out of 24. Your work hours should be a function of your total energy capacity. People who work hard but do not know how to play equally hard, are often unbalanced leaders. Their value systems get distorted and that leads to the demonstration of wrong values within the organization. For an obvious example, people with different and lower energy levels may work long hours with no value to the organization yet do exceptional harm to themselves and their private lives.

Playing hard should not mean, necessarily, jogging and keeping fit in the gymnasium so that you can work longer hours for the organization. It means having a social life, going to the theatre or having meals with friends, or all the other myriad interests which make people into more rounded human beings. Many of your subordinates are probably having high-quality social lives. A distorted social life for the strategic leader means he is less of a human being than the people around him. They will notice that and they will judge you accordingly. More importantly, you should judge yourself in the same light. If you find that you do not like playing, or you do not enjoy a private social life, it is also possible that you are a dull being who is probably not very good at strategy, leadership, or management. "Play" is what "earning a living" is for. Playing well enables us to be serious at work, although the luckiest people are those who find work as much fun as play.

Last word on luck

Occasionally, one hears leaders say that they have had a lot of bad luck and that things are just not going their way or coming out right for the organization. If you ever hear yourself saying those words you should ask yourself whether the problem is luck or you. Under most circumstances, the answer is *you*. If it is you, do you have the courage to leave the organization? Or demote yourself to the level where you used to be competent? If ever you have a disinclination to "do the right thing" remember, there may well be many thousands of workers below you who need those jobs much more than you need yours.

Lady Luck be with you! Work hard, and she'll be with you much more frequently.

Additional reading for this chapter

J. Adair, *Effective Leadership*, Pan, London, 1988

Myers I. Briggs with P. B. Myers, *MBTI Gifts Differing*, Consulting Psychologists Press, Palo Alto, 1980

S. R. Covey, *The 7 Habits of Highly Successful People*, Fireside (Simon & Schuster), New York, 1990

J. Heider, *The Tao of Leadership*, Gower, Aldershot, 1993

D. Keirsey and M. Bates, *Please Understand Me* (5th edn), Prometheus Nemesis Book Co., Del Mar, 1984

C. Levicki, *The Leadership Gene*, Financial Times Pitman Publishing, London, 1998

L. D. Ryan, *Clinical Interpretation of the FIRO-B*, Consulting Psychologists Press, Oxford, 1989

Conclusion

I hope you have enjoyed this book and that it has shown you how to complete a strategic analysis. It should also have demonstrated some of the ways that implementation can go well or badly. I hope you have used the book as a workbook and completed the audit pages as you read the chapters. There is a version of the complete workout system after this conclusion. Use it either as a check on your previous analysis or perhaps as a revision next year to see how the strategic purpose of your organization is moving along.

It is our intention to continuously improve this workout book in the light of new research and methodology as it evolves from the best business schools and organizations around the world. We continuously learn from experience and try to improve every aspect of the technique.

Good luck with your strategy. It is the most important thing you will ever do for your organization.

Dr Cyril J. Levicki, 1999

Part Four

"COOLING DOWN GENTLY"

Now measure your final strategy
workout fitness

Test your New Understanding
with a Final Workout

Hopefully you have reached this part of the book and are still interested in defining strategy for your organization. You will have understood from Part Three that it is harder to implement strategy than to analyze it. However, you are still determined to press on. You are determined to avoid the mistakes of your peers as outlined in Chapter 11. You have learnt all the lessons of Chapter 12 and know how to avoid hubris, the dangers of ego, and the need to communicate the strategy continuously to have any chance of success.

Our last piece of advice before you start communicating is to have the humility to check it all out once again. On the following pages are all the workout pages set out together. Complete them again, in the light of your "fitter" feel for the niceties and complexities of the whole subject.

If you are really fit for strategy you will almost certainly only need a few minutes now.

All the workouts are also supplied on CD in the back of this book.

THE MISSION WORKOUT

Complete the following mission audit questions.

What is the vision of the leader of the organization?
(Where is he taking the organization in the long run?)

_____

_____

_____

What core competencies need to be obtained?

_____

_____

_____

What will the organization look like in five years' time?

_____

_____

_____

THE EXTERNAL ENVIRONMENT WORKOUT

What are the most important economic factors in the organization's domestic market?

1 _____   2 _____

3 _____   4 _____

What are the most important economic factors in markets abroad?

1 _____   2 _____

3 _____   4 _____

What are the most important political factors likely to affect the organization?

1 _____   2 _____

3 _____   4 _____

Which legal factors affect or could affect the organization?

1 _____   2 _____

3 _____   4 _____

Which current demographic trends may affect the organization's workforce?

1 _____   2 _____

3 _____   4 _____

What are the trends in demand for the organization's main services or products?

1 _____   2 _____

3 _____   4 _____

Is there any key political legislation which could affect your industry(ies)?

1 _____   2 _____

3 _____   4 _____

THE COMPETITOR ANALYSIS WORKOUT

Current Industry Competitors

Under each category below, put in the names of companies or people where appropriate. Regard this as a simple measure of your knowledge of the industry.

Which are the top performers in your industry?

1 _____ 2 _____

3 _____ 4 _____

Are there any other important national competitors?

1 _____ 2 _____

3 _____ 4 _____

Who are the strategically most dangerous people in competing organizations?

1 _____ 2 _____

3 _____ 4 _____

Which are the important regional or local competitors?

1 _____ 2 _____

3 _____ 4 _____

Which are the current customers most likely to integrate backward?

1 _____ 2 _____

3 _____ 4 _____

Which are the current suppliers most likely to integrate forward?

1 _____ 2 _____

3 _____ 4 _____

Any organizations which might enter the industry?

1 _____ 2 _____

3 _____ 4 _____

THE INDIVIDUAL COMPETITOR PROFILE WORKOUT

Complete one of these for each important competitor mentioned on the previous page.

What is the competitor's company name? _____

What is its annual revenue and its annual profit? _____

What is the name of the competitor's leader? _____

What is his psychology? _____

Is the competitor satisfied with its current position in the industry?
Yes/No

If not, what strategic moves do you think it will make?

_____

_____

What action from your organization will provoke the fiercest retaliation?

_____

_____

What are the competitor's most important strengths?

_____

_____

What are the competitor's most important weaknesses?

_____

_____

STRENGTHS, NEUTRALS, AND WEAKNESSES WORKOUT

Check each of the following categories in terms of it being a strength, neutral, or a weakness.

Sometimes it helps to allocate a number from 1 to 5 indicating high (5), medium (3), or low (1). Thus, a Neutral with a 5 on it would be very close to a Strength with a 1 on the same category.

Organization function	Strength	Neutral	Weakness
Accounting skills (financial)	❑	❑	❑
Accounting skills (management)	❑	❑	❑
Access to finance	❑	❑	❑
Business strategy	❑	❑	❑
Corporate strategy	❑	❑	❑
Cost structure of business	❑	❑	❑
Distribution network	❑	❑	❑
Divisional strategy	❑	❑	❑
Entry barriers	❑	❑	❑
Exit barriers	❑	❑	❑
Information technology	❑	❑	❑
Innovation (turning research into products)	❑	❑	❑
Lateral communication	❑	❑	❑
Leader's ability	❑	❑	❑
Leadership in general	❑	❑	❑
Loyalty of workforce	❑	❑	❑
Management ability	❑	❑	❑
Manufacturing skills	❑	❑	❑
Marketing skills	❑	❑	❑
Organization structure	❑	❑	❑
Products	❑	❑	❑
Quality of brands	❑	❑	❑
Quality of staff	❑	❑	❑

STRENGTHS, NEUTRALS, AND WEAKNESSES

WORKOUT (cont.)

Organization function	Strength	Neutral	Weakness
Reputation in market	❏	❏	❏
Reputation as employer	❏	❏	❏
Relationship with government	❏	❏	❏
Relationship with regulator	❏	❏	❏
Relationship with trade unions	❏	❏	❏
Relationships with suppliers	❏	❏	❏
Research and development	❏	❏	❏
Services	❏	❏	❏
Selling skills	❏	❏	❏
Technical engineering skills	❏	❏	❏
Personnel administration	❏,	❏	❏
Vertical communication	❏	❏	❏

Additional categories
(*Relevant to your particular business*)

	Strength	Neutral	Weakness
_____	❏	❏	❏
_____	❏	❏	❏
_____	❏	❏	❏

SUMMARY OF SNW WORKOUT

Select the top four strengths, neutrals, and weaknesses from your analysis on the previous audit pages and set them out below with a brief note on how you might use, neutralize, or improve the effects of each on the success of the organization's mission.

The strengths

1 _____

2 _____

3 _____

4 _____

The neutrals

1 _____

2 _____

3 _____

4 _____

The weaknesses

1 _____

2 _____

3 _____

4 _____

THE CULTURE WORKOUT

Culture is "the way we do things around here." Complete each of the following categories with the most important features under each category. It is important to note the effect of each subject. E.g. for past leaders, put their name – but also what behaviors remain in the organization because of the way they did things when they were the leader.

HISTORY

List the important events in the organization's history.

Event 1 _____

Effect of event 1 _____

_____

Event 2 _____

Effect of event 2 _____

_____

Event 3 _____

Effect of event 3 _____

_____

What is the most important feature of the mental environment?

_____

_____

What is its cultural effect? _____

_____

THE CULTURE WORKOUT (cont.)

LEADERSHIP ISSUES

1 The past leader

Name the most memorable past leader _____

What behavior is still attributable to him/her?_____

_____

2 The current leader

Name the current main leader _____

What particular qualities do you associate with him/her?_____

_____

What is the physical environment of head office?_____

_____

What is the physical environment of the rest of the organization?_____

_____

TECHNOLOGY OF THE ORGANIZATION

Which of the following technologies applies to the organization?
(Check whichever one of the following pairs applies to your organization.)

☐ **Paper based**	or	☐ **Computer based**
☐ **Batch technology**	or	☐ **Process technology**
☐ **National scale of operations**	or	☐ **International scale**
☐ **Mature industries**	or	☐ **New industries**
☐ **Product**	or	☐ **Service**

**What culture effect does each of those you have checked off have upon
the organization?** _____

_____

_____

THE CULTURE WORKOUT (cont.)

The way people behave in the organization is learned through the stories and anecdotes they hear when they join and while they remain. Try to think of those which have affected the way you behave:

MYTHS *(These are stories which are probably untrue but which get told anyway.)*

What is the best known myth in the organization?

_____

_____

LEGENDS *(These are stories which have sources long buried in the past, but which get passed on anyway, with variations.)*

What is the best known legend in the organization?

_____

_____

STORIES *(These are just the probably true stories you are told to explain how to do things around here.)*

What is the best known story in the organization?

_____

_____

ANECDOTES *(These are entertaining stories which also teach.)*

What is the best known anecdote in the organization?

_____

_____

VALUE CHAIN ANALYSIS WORKOUT

Refer to p.250. Find your business's current position(s) in the value chain(s) of its main products and services.

Fill in the vertical opportunities for products and services currently being supplied by competitors.

Complete the backwards and forwards integration opportunities from the point of view of:

1 Attitude of customers.
2 Availability of business to purchase or copiability of competitors.
3 Profit margins.
4 Your business's competencies and alignment with the desired strategic direction.

	Stage One *Finding raw materials*	Stage Two *Manufacture of components*	Stage Three *Assembly of final product*	Stage Four *Wholesale distribution*	Stage Five *Retail to final user*
Typical profit level range	%	%	%	%	%
Typical risk	Low/Medium/High	Low/Medium/High	Low/Medium/High	Low/Medium/High	Low/Medium/High
Key factor					

LONG-TERM STRATEGY WORKOUT

What competing products and/or services would you like in your own business's portfolio?

_____

_____

Are there any competitors you might like to take over which are available or buyable? Name them.

_____

_____

Are there any suppliers, making superior profit margins to your own business, which you could effectively take over *and* successfully manage? Name them.

_____

_____

Should the firm grow, remain stable, or diminish in size?_____

Which parts of the business should:

Focus?   Differentiate?   Be an industry cost leader?

_____   _____   _____

_____   _____   _____

_____   _____   _____

_____   _____   _____

LONG-TERM STRATEGY WORKOUT (cont.)

What are the organization's main objectives over which time horizons?

Only complete the time horizons relevant to your organization or your part of the organization. Ignore time horizons which are too long for you to contemplate. Name the new areas of interest of the business and state your overall revenue and profit targets for each stage.

10 years _____

_____

_____

_____

5 years _____

_____

_____

_____

4 years _____

_____

_____

_____

3 years _____

_____

_____

_____

2 years _____

_____

_____

_____

ORGANIZATIONAL STRUCTURE WORKOUT

What is the size of the organization?
People? _____ Revenue? _____ Profits? _____

What geographical area does it cover?
Local? _____ Regional? _____ Country? _____ International? _____

Does the organization provide many or a few services or products? _____

Which is better known?
The company name? _____ The brand names of the products? _____

Is the organization currently centralized? _____ or decentralized? _____

Are there lots of rules? _____ Or very few rules? _____

What is the proportion of managers to workers? _____

How do you communicate?
Verbally? _____ Written messages? _____ Electronic mail? _____

Does the organization offer the same service all the time? _____

Does almost every order require a different process? _____

How is the organization structured now?
Functional ☐   Geographical ☐   Product ☐   Matrix ☐   Mixed ☐

What is the average span of control (span of control = the number of people managed by each manager), at each level in the hierarchy of the business?

_____

Are there rational reasons for the differences between levels in the hierarchy?

_____

ORGANIZATIONAL STRUCTURE WORKOUT (cont.)

How many direct supports does the leader have?

_____

What is the total number of employees?

_____

What is the total number of operators, meaning people with direct "doing" jobs?

_____

What is the total number of supervisors and managers?_____

Can you design a structure which decreases the number of managers?

_____

_____

What are the major advantages of your design?

_____

_____

What are the major disadvantages of your design?

_____

_____

Please think about all the answers you have written above. Although they will not give an automatic answer, they will guide you to the way one could ideally structure the organization.

SHORT-TERM TACTICS WORKOUT

Part One – The Short-Term Targets

Using the highlighted problems from the workout sheet from Chapter 5 (see p.87), as well as the long-term strategic targets, especially the two and three-year strategies decide the key three or four measurable objectives that must be achieved this year to ensure that the organization is on track for the long-term mission.

Priority 1 _____

_____

Measure _____

_____

Priority 2 _____

_____

Measure _____

_____

Priority 3 _____

_____

Measure _____

_____

Priority 4 _____

_____

Measure _____

_____

Part Two – The Accounts

To get your tactics into context

Corporation/business/department's total revenue	$/£m	_____
Operating profits	$/£m	_____
Profits before tax	$/£m	_____
This year's profit as percent of net revenue	%	_____
Cash flow	$/£m	_____
Assets	$/£m	_____

Budget for your department

(Complete the lines which are relevant to you.)

Total expenditure	$/£	_____
Total costs	$/£	_____
Total sales	$/£	_____
Budgeted profit/loss	$/£	_____
Total number of subordinates in the department at beginning of year		_____
Total number of subordinates in the department at end of year		_____
Total bonus for department	$/£	_____

Targets against which the bonus is set

1 _____   2 _____

3 _____   4 _____

Additional Reading Materials
mentioned throughout the Book

J. Adair, *Effective Leadership*, Pan, London, 1988

R. Adams, J. Carruthers, and S. Hamil, *Changing Corporate Values*, Kogan Page, London, 1991

M. Belbin, *Team Roles at Work*, Butterworth-Heinemann, Oxford, 1993

M. Belbin, *Management Team – Why They Succeed or Fail*, Butterworth-Heinemann, Oxford, 1991

K. Blanchard and S. Johnson, *The One Minute Manager*, William Collins, Glasgow, 1990

I. Briggs Myers with P. B. Myers, *MBTI Gifts Differing*, Consulting Psychologists Press, California, 1980

T. Burns and G. M. Stalker, *The Management of Innovation*, Tavistock, London, 1961

A. Campbell, M. Devine, and D. Young, *A Sense of Mission*, Hutchinson, London, 1990

A. P. Chandler, *Strategy & Structure*, MIT Press, Boston, 1962

S. R. Covey, *The 7 Habits of Highly Successful People*, Fireside (Simon & Schuster), New York, 1990

T. E. Deal and A. A. Kennedy, *Corporate Cultures*, Addison-Wesley, Reading, Massachusetts, 1982

R. M. Grant, *Contemporary Strategy Analysis*, Blackwell, Oxford, 1995

G. Hamel and C. K. Pralahad, *Competing for the Future*, Harvard Business School Press, Boston, 1994

C. Handy, *Understanding Organisations* (4th edn), Penguin, Harmondsworth, Middlesex, 1993

J. Heider, *The Tao of Leadership*, Gower, Aldershot, 1993

J. Hunt, *Managing People at Work*, Pan, London, 1981

E. Jacques, *Measurement of Responsibility*, Tavistock, London, 1956

E. Jacques, *Time Span Handbook*, Heinemann, London, 1964

J. Kay, *Foundations of Corporate Success*, Oxford University Press, Oxford, 1993

D. Keirsey and M. Bates, *Please Understand Me* (5th edn), Prometheus Nemesis Book Co., Palo Alto, 1984

P. R. Lawrence, *Managing Differentiation and Integration*, Harvard University Press, Boston, 1967

C. J. Levicki, *The Leadership Gene*, Financial Times Pitman Publishing, London, 1998

J. G. March, *Decisions & Organisations*, Blackwell, Oxford, 1988

J. G. March and H. A. Simon, *Organisations*, Wiley & Sons, New York, 1958

T. J. Peters and R. H. Waterman, *In Search of Excellence*, Harper & Row, New York, 1982

T. Peters and N. Austin, *A Passion for Excellence*, William Collins & Sons, Glasgow, 1985

M. E. Porter, *Competitive Advantage*, Free Press, New York, 1985

M. E. Porter, *Competitive Strategy*, Free Press, New York, 1980

D. Pugh (ed.), *Organisation Theory*, Penguin, Harmondsworth, 1971

D. S. Pugh and D. J. Hickson, *Organisational Structure in its Context*, Saxon House/Lexington Books, D. E. Heath, Farnborough, 1976

P. Q. Quinn, *Intelligent Enterprise*, Free Press, New York, 1992

S. P. Robbins, *Training in Interpersonal Skills*, Prentice-Hall, Englewood Cliffs, New Jersey, 1989

L. D. Ryan, *Clinical Interpretation of the FIRO-B*, Consulting Psychologists Press, Oxford, 1989

S. Slatter, *Corporate Recovery*, Penguin, Harmondsworth, Middlesex, 1984

F. Trompenaars, *Riding the Waves of Cufture*, Economist Books, London, 1993

H. Vroom and E. L. Deci, *Management & Motivation*, Penguin, Harmondsworth, Middlesex, 1979

O. Williamson, *Markets & Hierarchies*, Free Press, New York, 1975

J. Woodward, *Industrial Organisation Theory and Practice*, Oxford University Press, London, 1965

J. Woodward (ed.), *Industrial Organisation, Behaviour & Control*, Oxford University Press, London, 1970

Index

integrating backward 55, 60
and mission statements 17, 20–1
see also captive companies

Dauphin Distribution 100
demography 43, 45, 47, 240
Deutsche Telecom 37
differentiation strategies 74–5, 132,
    137–8, 141, 147, 251
diminishing strategies *see*
    retrenchment
distribution function 32–3, 43, 55–6,
    76, 87, 112–14, 116–117, 118–19,
    120, 123, 124, 125–6, 130, 156,
    179, 250
divestment 136
Dixon's 43

economic trends 35–7, 46, 240
economies of scale 38, 46
employees 10, 23, 45, 72, 88, 100,
    102, 152, 153–4, 169, 179, 184,
    215, 244, 253–4, 256
  attitude surveys 85
  laying off 19–20, 105–106, 177, 210
  mobility 81, 119
  motivation and loyalty 11, 17, 19,
    23, 24, 71, 79, 87, 154, 159–60,
    174, 182, 193, 207–8, 220, 243
  quality and standards 82, 87, 97,
    243
  recruiting 17, 19, 83, 88, 177, 179
  skills 19, 38–9, 55, 67, 88, 112, 134,
    145, 155–8, 177, 181, 222
  time horizons 140–1, 143
  training and development 8, 71,
    154–9, 161, 177–8, 181, 222–3
  treatment of 19–21, 88, 96, 97, 190
  wages 45, 190
  working conditions 23, 42–4

see also vertical communications
  under
  communications
entertainment industry 52, 56,
    115–16
entry and exit barriers 40–1, 76–7,
    85, 87, 117, 118, 120, 122, 125,
    243
environment, physical 42, 46, 101–2,
    109, 247
ethics 6, 23, 83, 94, 96, 208, 228–30
EU (European Union) 33, 41, 42, 43,
    58–9
exit barriers *see* entry and exit
    barriers
external environment analysis 7, 9,
    27–47, 29, 31, 51, 69, 97, 145
  workout paper 47

Federal Express 19, 41–2
finance function 73, 74–6 87, 136,
    155, 174–5, 180–1, 184, 206, 243
  workout paper 256
FIRO-B tests 209–10
focus strategies 132, 139, 251
Ford Motor Company 37, 45
France 32, 37, 46
France Télécom 37
functional structures 155–7, 156, 159,
    168, 253

gas industry 44
see also British Gas, Transco
Gates, Bill 9
GEC 9
General Motors 45
geographical structures 152, 158–9,
    168, 253
Germany 37
  see also Porsche, VW

market share 19, 22, 43–4, 54, 126, 133–5, 178

Marks & Spencer 106–7, 122, 137

Marriott 37

Marshall, Sir Colin 10

matrix structures 159–61, 168, 253

Maxwell, Robert 105–6

Meridian 37

Microsoft 9, 19, 37–8, 52, 57–8, 97, 102

missions and mission statements def 17, 7, 17–24, 23, 173, 178, 215
    drawing up 21–2
    subdividing 216–17
    workout papers 25, 239

Mitsubishi 37

Morita, Akio 20

Murdoch, Rupert 52–3

myths and legends 104, 104, 110, 248

NASA 18

National Freight Company 118

National Cash Registers 21

national cultural differences 32, 41–2

neutrals 65, 67–8, 71, 87–9, 133, 145, 243, 245

Nissan 37

objectives 6–7, 11, 22, 148

organizational analysis 7, 10, 63–89, 145, 239
    direction of movement 21, 25, 94
    rate of change 69
    reputation 82–3, 88, 244

organizational culture 7, 69, 91–110, 133, 145, 177
    and history 95–6, 108, 246
    mental atmosphere 96–8, 108, 227–8, 246
    workout papers 108–10, 246–8

organizational structures def 151, 7, 81, 87, 149–69, 202, 206–7, 223, 243
    informal 161–2, 162–3
    re-engineering 71, 74, 177, 223–5
    workout papers 168–9, 253–4
    see also functional structures, geographical structures, matrix structures, product structures

out-sourcing 80

patents 121

pharmaceutical industry 43, 57, 84–5, 122, 125, 165

politics and regulation 29, 32–3, 35, 43–4, 47, 55, 85, 88, 119, 240, 244
    influencing 43–5, 53, 80–1, 83–4

Porsche 46

prices
    competition 45, 54, 137, 138
    raising 137, 138–9, 146

privatization 84

Procter & Gamble 77

production 155–6
    final product assembly 113–14, 116–18, 120–5, 130, 250
    productivity 179–80
    product life-cycles 35–6, 46–7, 80
    product range 81, 87

product structures 157–9, 168, 253

profitability 23, 44, 83–6, 113, 157

profits and margins 35–42, 61, 85, 112, 115, 116, 118–19, 120–2, 124, 129–130, 133, 145, 147–8, 168, 179, 184, 249, 251, 253, 256
    decrease in 125
    maximizing 178, 180–1
    and value chain 123, 125–6

project teams 160–1

How you can get the most from your

Strategy Workout

A Note from the Author

I developed the techniques of the workout over many years of practical strategy analysis with leaders of organizations. It may help you to know my modus operandi.

I am usually introduced to an organization's leader by another leader who has used my services, or as the result of a television or radio appearance, or as a consequence of somebody reading a book or article I have written.

When I meet the leader, I try to ascertain whether we like each other, have similar values and ethics and can tell each other the truth. If this all holds together, we usually then proceed to begin the exercise of strategy analysis shown in this book.

I usually send the workout book to all the subordinates who will be participating in the strategy appraisal or change. I ask them to complete the workout before they come to a seminar. We usually then have a three-day seminar where we work through each workout sheet, one by one, until we have complete agreement on the analysis of the essentials of the strategy.

After the seminar, the leader, usually with my help, writes up the new mission and strategy and distributes it throughout the organization, to ensure full communication and understanding. In particularly large organizations, we might involve as many as 50 or 70 senior executives in the exercise over several three-day seminars. It is a remarkably effective way of finding new strategic paths and achieving consensus on the future direction.

We appreciate that, by its very nature, this book is now probably looking a little over used. We have asked you to use it as a strategy workbook and now it is covered in your notes and ideas. Therefore, we are giving you a special offer if you wish to purchase a clean copy. This order form entitles you to a discount on your next purchase of *The Strategy Workout*. Simply fill in the details below and return it to your local bookseller or, for postal orders, please send to:

Pearson Education, DEPT CS, FREEPOST, Pearson Education Distribution Centre, Slaidburn Crescent, Fylde Road, Southport, PR9 9BR. Tel: 01704 508080 Fax: 01704 506685

Your details

Mr/Mrs/Ms/Miss Initial _____   Surname _____

Job title_____

Department _____

Company _____

Address _____

_____

_____

Postcode _____ Tel No _____

Please send me _____ copy/ies of *The Strategy Workout* ISBN 0273 64433 5./RRP £22.99; special price £19.99.

Postage charges

UK please add £3.00 per order

Elsewhere in Europe please add £5.00 per order

Rest of the World please add £9.00 per order

(one payment per order – whether you order 1 copy or 20)

Payment details

I enclose a cheque made payable to Pearson Education for (total) £ _____

Please debit my Access/Visa/Barclaycard/Mastercard/AmEx/Switch/Diners for (total) £ _____

Card No ☐ ☐ ☐ ☐ ☐ ☐ ☐ ☐ ☐ ☐ ☐ ☐ ☐ ☐ ☐ ☐ ☐ ☐ ☐

Expiry date _____   Issue No (for Switch only) _____

Signature _____   Date _____

Please note that prices are subject to change without notification, please call to check the current price of the book.